Nailed It! 2

7 Easy Steps to
Nail Your UC Prompts

ROXANNE OCAMPO

Nailed It! 2

7 Easy Steps to Nail Your UC Prompts

Title ID: 8850867

ISBN- 978-1723436246

Cover illustration Will Orozco

Author Photo Laura Bravo Mertz (Solifoto)

Limit of Liability/Disclaimer of Warranty

Dedication

This book is dedicated to every student

with an extraordinary story to tell.

Put truth to your words.

Own your awesomeness.

Show them what you're made of.

We're counting on you.

Other books by
Dr. Roxanne Ocampo

Nailed it!

Quetzal Mama's Toolkit
for Extraordinary College Essays

Winner 2016 Best Educational Young Adult Book

International Latino Book Awards

Flight of the Quetzal Mama:

How to Raise Latino Superstars
and Get Them Into the Best Colleges

El Vuelo de la Mamá Quetzal:

Cómo Criar Hijos Exitosos y
Prepararlos para las Mejores Universidades

Betcha Didn't Know!

Quetzal Mama's Tips
for *Latino* Parents

Table of Contents

Acknowledgments

The Quetzal Mama Scholars whose spirit of generosity

compelled them to share their essays in this book.

Thank you for paying it forward.

Your stories will influence and inspire future Latinx students

to apply *successfully* to the University of California.

Abrazos.

Lili Castillo

Yesica Chaparro

Arleth Aparicio Flores

Josue Cuauhtémoc Hernandez

Alejandrina Lopez

Sara Reyes Luna

Brionna Martinez

Leslie Romo

Special thanks to students I coached during the last two

UC admission cycles who allowed me to share their

Personal Insight Questions. *Mil gracias.*

About the Author

Dr. Roxanne Ocampo is a national college admissions expert and proud *mamá latina*. She is the author of five award-winning non-fiction books (available *en Español*) focused on college admissions. As Founder & CEO of Quetzal Mama™ – she has coached more than 10,000 students since 2010. She runs the Quetzal Mama Scholars Program, a year-long, intensive college admissions program for students in San Diego County. She conducts workshops and boot camps throughout the U.S. focused on college admission strategies.

Her workshops cover K-5, middle school, and high school strategies for college admission and competitive scholarships. The students from her practice have earned admission to the most prestigious universities as well as national scholarship awards. Her writing expertise is also informed by teaching English Composition for college students.

Dr. Ocampo earned a Doctorate of Education in 2017 from the University of California at San Diego, where she received a full fellowship. Her Dissertation and research topic was *"Undermatching"* of low-income, first-generation, high performing, Latino students. Her Dissertation was recognized with a $1,000 cash prize at the 2018 Outstanding Dissertation Awards at the AAHHE Conference. She holds a Master's Degree and Bachelor's Degree in English from California State University East Bay. The theories and philosophy that guide her teaching and publications are situated in Critical Race Theory. She was born and raised in the Bay Area (San José) and resides in San Marcos, California. Her work has been featured on ABC News, Good Day Sacramento, and Sacramento & Co.

Roxanne is married to Dr. Arturo E. Ocampo—an expert in Diversity & Inclusion and a Civil Rights, Immigrant Rights, and Education Law Attorney. Together they have raised three phenomenal *hijos* – Carlos José (UC Santa Cruz Class of 2015), Gabriella (Harvard Class of 2015 & Harvard Medical School Class of 2020), and Emilio (Cornell University, "Future" Class of 2023).

Introduction

I created this lightweight "pocketbook" for you to grab and go. I wanted to give you a portable toolkit to throw in your backpack or read while on the bus. Each chapter is a super condensed, straight-to-the-point summary to help you quickly understand key points. *Tambien*, I've created a Kindle version (electronic) of this book for students who prefer a digital copy.

It's also lightweight because I go straight to 7 critical strategies, helping you nail your essays as quickly as possible. While there are a million ways you can structure your PIQ's, I share the structure that's proven successful for the majority of students I've coached in the last 7 years. This structure helps students quickly and effectively tell their story and *nail* their essays.

The students I coach who use these methods will finish all 4 drafts of their UC Personal Insight Questions (PIQs) within 1 hour and 30 minutes. Yep, 4 essays in an hour and a half. And, it doesn't matter if the students are English Learners, AP English superstars, or somewhere in the middle. These steps work.

Although I host 2-day UC Essay Writing Boot Camps throughout California, I wanted to create this toolkit to help students who are unable to attend these in-person camps. I took content directly from the camps and synthesized to share in a concise way.

School districts, non-profits, teachers, counselors, college-going organizations, TRIO programs, and anyone invested in helping our students gain admission to a University of California campus will find this book a helpful tool in working with our students. I offer bulk purchase discounts to organizations who gift this toolkit to their students. *¡Llámame!*

If you're a student and want to bring Quetzal Mama to host a UC Essay Writing Boot Camp *for free* at your high school campus, contact me at <u>quetzalmama@gmail.com</u>.

I'm excited to be working with you at this pivotal moment in your college journey. Now go *nail* those UC prompts!

¡Si se puede!

—Quetzal Mama

1

Overview of the Personal Insight Prompts (PIQ's)

Why the PIQ's?

*I*f you've already submitted test scores, uploaded transcripts, and populated your UC application, why are the UC people now asking you to write 4 essays? Don't they already know everything about you? Can't they see your absolute brilliance already? Well actually, no. They only know statistical information such as GPA and class rank, or your percentile on the ACT or SAT. And, they can only make inferences from your extra-curricular activities, leadership, or community service.

But, they won't know **why** or **how** you did what you did. For example, why did you choose to be an officer in MEChA? Why did you spend 10 hours per week tutoring students at the local elementary school? What motivated you to take 6 AP courses? Why do you want to attend a UC versus a private school or your local state college? They can't get that from your application. You have to *tell* them.

You Have to *Tell Them*

Unique Experiences & Obstacles – In addition to statistical information (grades, rank, test scores, etc.) regarding school performance and activities, the UC people want to know about your unique experiences and obstacles. Did any barriers or obstacles impact your pathway to college? For example, how would the UC people know why your application is missing after- school sports, clubs, or activities? How would they know your parents work non-traditional shifts, and that you're responsible for taking care of your siblings after school? Or, how would they know you're part of the Migrant Education program and their bus pulls up at 3:00pm to take you home? Maybe you couldn't qualify for the medical summer institute because of your undocumented status? The UC folks won't know this simply by looking at your application. This context must be addressed in your essays. Again, you have to *tell* them.

Context – Lastly, the UC people want context. They want to know how you achieved academic excellence based on resources, institutions, and mentors available (or not) to you. For example, if you're killing it in AP Calculus yet neither of your parents took math beyond arithmetic, they want to know how you did it. If only 4% of students in your high school graduate and meet the A–G requirements, how did you make it into that 4%? If no one in your family has attended a 4-year university, what motivated you to push yourself to be the first one? If you live in a rural area and you had to spend 2.5 hours each way traveling to your high school, they want to know.

Context also lets the UC people know why you did certain things. For example, why did you spend 250 volunteer hours for a program serving special needs students? Maybe you have a younger sister with special needs, and your experiences with helping your sister influenced your decision to volunteer for that organization. How would the UC's know *why* or *what* motivated you to invest this time?

Context also matters when it comes to your academic performance. If there are no Advanced Placement courses available to you, and you took it upon yourself to enroll in summer courses at the local community college . . . how would the UC readers know your reasons for doing so? Unless you tell them, they will simply make an educated guess. The Personal Insight Questions also help you address things like:

- Why you developed passion for a particular subject like science, engineering, etc.;
- How your racial/ethnic/cultural background influenced your academic journey;
- The unique skills, talents, passion, characteristics, traits, attributes, strengths, and disposition that separate you from other candidates.

Now that you know *why* the UC people are asking you to write 4 PIQ's, let's look at the general instructions.

General Instructions

There are 8 potential UC prompts referred to as *Personal Insight Questions (PIQ's)*. Don't be intimidated by these 8 prompts – think of them as 8 options to showcase your awesomeness. I often substitute the word, "Questions" with "Opportunities." You have 8 opportunities to sell your story. You'll need to respond to 4 of the 8 prompts (no, you can't "opt out"). Each essay has a word limit of 350 words. Use all 350 words. Yep, do it. That's really not a lot of words. It's only about a half page of a standard 8.5 x 11 piece of paper. Here are the 8 PIQ's:

University of California PIQ's

1. Describe an example of your leadership experience in which you have positively influenced others, helped resolve disputes or contributed to group efforts over time.

2. Every person has a creative side, and it can be expressed in many ways: problem solving, original and innovative thinking, and artistically, to name a few. Describe how you express your creative side.

3. What would you say is your greatest talent or skill? How have you developed and demonstrated that talent over time?

4. Describe how you have taken advantage of a significant educational opportunity or worked to overcome an educational barrier you have faced.

5. Describe the most significant challenge you have faced and the steps you have taken to overcome this challenge. How has this challenge affected your academic achievement?

6. Think about an academic subject that inspires you. Describe how you have furthered this interest inside and/or outside of the classroom.

7. What have you done to make your school or your community a better place?

8. Beyond what has already been shared in your application, what do you believe makes you stand out as a strong candidate for admissions to the University of California?

The Most Important Prompts?

Which of the 8 prompts is the most important? Which will yield you the greatest admission odds? Which prompt do the UC readers value most?

ALL OF THEM. Don't be fooled. There are no particular "preferred" or "advantageous" prompts admission readers favor. They are all equally weighted. The extent you will nail your prompt will be determined by your content, theme, structure, and strategies. That's why you're reading this book. *Que no?*

How is it Used?

I'm a HUGE fan of the University of California for many reasons. No, they don't pay me to say that. I say this because I want to hug them for many reasons. One reason is the way they evaluate and admit students. They use a "holistic" approach or "comprehensive review" in screening applicants. This means your *entire* student profile will be considered – both your unique background and academic statistics.

It means you won't be unfairly compared to a student from a super affluent community who attended a highly resourced high school, had access to test prep programs, private tutors, a comprehensive AP program, and parents who likely hold graduate level degrees (and have themselves navigated the complex selective college process).

It means even though you went to a super affluent high school campus – a boarding school, private school, Catholic, etc., -- but you got there by working your tail off and earning a full scholarship, they're all over that. The holistic review has got you covered.

It means your application will be reviewed in light of what you achieved given the resources (or lack thereof) you were provided, obstacles you navigated, and barriers you faced along your academic pathway. Totally fair.

But hold up! This doesn't mean "minority" students are assessed with "special" criteria (aka lower academic standards). *This is a myth*. Let me be clear – the University of California has an academic benchmark students must meet to be considered for admission, period. However, once students have met that benchmark, they'll be assessed based on the context of their academic achievements. To understand how the holistic review process works, consider the backgrounds of the following two candidates:

Candidate A (we'll call her Marisol) is a student who attends Greenfield High School – a coastal town in Monterey County, California where 97% of students are Hispanic, more than 80% are considered socioeconomically disadvantaged, 1 in 3 are English Learners, and only 7% of graduating seniors meet A-G requirements. That means, only 7% of these students have met the *minimum* criteria to be eligible for a UC campus. Marisol will be the first in her family to attend college. She holds a 3.85 GPA, 1250 composite SAT score, 27 composite ACT score, and there is only 1 counselor for every 523 students at her school. Marisol's Personal Insight Questions reflect how she acted as a surrogate parent for her four younger siblings so that her single-parent mother could work a graveyard shift. She performed more than 400 hours of community service, tutoring migrant education students in math and science. Her life objective is to become a Legal Aid attorney in

California to assist low-income residents with housing and employment rights.

Candidate B (we'll call her Madison) is a student from the affluent Menlo-Atherton suburb of Northern California and attends an exclusive boarding school staffed with traditional counselors *and* college advisors. Both of Madison's parents hold graduate degrees from Ivy League institutions. Her parents have paid for her to attend the Princeton Review SAT test prep program, hired private tutors, and hired a private essay-writing coach to help Madison craft an exceptional essay. Since her freshman year in high school Madison travelled each summer to various countries in Europe, Asia, and Africa. She holds a 3.60 GPA, a composite SAT score of 1310, and a composite ACT score of 27. Madison's goal is to study journalism so that she can become a food blogger. Her Personal Statement reflects how her world view is influenced through summer vacations, eating interesting foods, and visiting museums throughout the world.

After reading these very different profiles you can see how unfair it would be to compare Candidate A to Candidate B. Thankfully, the UC's also agree it would be unfair. They realize it would be illogical and unfair to ignore factors such as financial resources, a family's academic background, and access to college-going capital in the context of academic achievement.

The following are the 14 factors the UC's consider when evaluating your application:

1. Grade-point average

2. Test scores

3. Performance in and number of courses beyond minimum a-g requirements

4. UC-approved honors courses and advanced courses

5. Eligibility in the Local Context (ELC) – CA residents only

6. Quality of senior-year program of study

7. Academic opportunities in California high schools

8. Outstanding performance in one or more academic subject areas

9. Achievements in special projects

10. Improvement in academic performance

11. Special talents, achievements and awards

12. Participation in educational preparation programs

13. Academic accomplishment in light of life experiences

14. Geographic location

Now that you understand how context plays a role, you can be assured the UC's will value the information you provide in your Personal Insight Questions.

Who Reads It?

In addition to the Admissions staff, additional readers may include faculty within your discipline; college admission consultants; alumni; and contracted essay readers unaffiliated with the University of California. These experienced essay readers will plow through each essay, evaluating and scoring *in three minutes or less*.

During the admissions recruitment cycle, readers will read essays all day, for months at a time. The readers will not know your name, but they will know important information about you such as how many students at your school receive Free & Reduced Lunch, how many AP courses are offered, etc. They will see your essay *and* your application together, so they can fairly review your potential in light of your demographic background.

Here's another reason I'm a big fan of the UC's. Their readers are highly trained to ensure each student's application is read fairly, aligned with a pre-defined rubric. More than one reader will evaluate your application, so that a single individual does not determine the outcome of any candidate's acceptance, waitlist, or denial. And, if the two readers have significantly different scores, your application is then taken to a third reader who is an expert. This third reader reviews your application and makes the final determination. I hope you can see why you shouldn't worry that one person may be biased "against" you and ruin your chances for admission.

PIQ's are Distinct from Traditional Essays

Because you'll be writing 4 essays with a cap of 350 words each, you'll need to approach the PIQ's in a somewhat non-traditional way. Unlike the Common Application prompts or essays you've written in AP English, you won't necessarily follow the same structure. There's simply not enough space.

When students ask me how to structure their responses, I tell them, *"Write it as if you were responding to an interview question."* At an interview, if a panel member asks you "Why are you the best person for this job?" you wouldn't wax philosophically about that memorable summer vacation in Oaxaca. You'd get right to the answer and provide a few impactful examples that support your answer. That's pretty much the strategy here in a nutshell.

Another way the PIQ's are distinct from other essays is that the UC people are asking for concrete details. **Two thirds of the 8 prompts** ask you to *describe* something. In other words, they want descriptive details about your experiences. They're not asking you to compare or contrast, or to analyze a scenario. They're asking you to speak in first person *describing* your personal background, experiences, and identity.

Recap

You'll select 4 prompts (out of 8 options).
All 8 prompts are equally weighted.
You must write 4 prompts (no opting out).
Each prompt is 350 words maximum.
Essay responses are like answering interview questions.
The UC's use a holistic approach when
reading your application.
Your PIQ's give the UC's *context.*
More than one reader will review your
application and essay.

2

7 Steps to Nail Your PIQ's

You Can Do This!

*T*ake a deep breath. Take a second to give yourself a big hug. I want you to put things in perspective for a moment. You're an academic SUPERSTAR. You've made it this far – being eligible to apply to one of the most rigorous, world renowned research institutions. You're likely in the top 15% of your graduating class, you've met all the A-G's, and took many AP or IB courses. You're seriously an academic Rockstar. Don't diminish your awesomeness. Own it.

Now, feel all the pride that comes with knowing this truth. Keep this truth in mind when you realize you're about to write one of most important essays of your life. Don't be scared though! Quetzal Mama is here and I've got your back. In fact, I've had the back of more than 10,000 students in the past 7 years and I've walked them through this same process. Many are anxious and afraid, feeling like they don't have the confidence or skills to write an excellent essay. However, they trusted this process and produced excellent essays. They often tell me, "I can't believe how easy that was!" Soon, you'll be saying the same.

The quickest and least stressful way to approach the PIQ's is to follow the 7 steps I've created below. I've designed these steps to help you get through the process one exercise at a time. That means you don't have to sit down and write the whole thing at once. It means you can work on Step 1, then go on to Step 2 a day or two later. By the time you've reached Step 7, you'll be amazed at the simplicity and quality of your completed prompts.

I want you to also realize that just because something seems simple doesn't mean it translates to inferior or lower quality essays. It's a simple process because I've streamlined this by working with thousands of students over the last 7 years. Trust the process. Trust Quetzal Mama. Trust you can do this.

The Rubric

There are millions of ways you can approach your PIQ's. However, from my expertise working with more than 10,000 students in the last 7 years, I can tell you nearly all of the students I've coached have adopted the rubric below. These students earned admission to the most selective UC campuses and received outstanding financial aid packages, including the coveted Regents' and Chancellors' Scholarship Award (top 1% of UC applicants).

This rubric provides a no-fail, sound structure, and covers all the bases. If you follow the 7 critical steps and use this rubric to structure your essay, you'll definitely nail it. Here are the steps:

Quetzal Mama's *7 Steps* to Nail your PIQ's

1 – *¡Eso!* Identify 4 Key Strengths

2 – *Dilo y Síguelo* Align Traits with PIQ's

3

Step #1 - ¡Eso!
Identify 4 Key Strengths

Deciding which of the 4 Personal Insight Questions (PIQ's) you'll select is challenging. How can you narrow the list and pick the 4 PIQ's that best speaks to your strengths, talents, and experiences? How can 4 prompts fully describe who you are and why you deserve a spot at the UC's?

The first step in deciding which of the 4 PIQs you'll select is to imagine your entire person – your academic profile; unique life experiences; hardships or obstacles; strengths; talents; and everything that has shaped your road to becoming a UC candidate. In describing this person, try to imagine the 4 most important qualities that fully describe *you*. To do this, I ask my students to envision their persona as 4 segments that make up a whole – just like a puzzle:

Surprisingly, this seems to be the most challenging task for nearly all students I coach. It's tough because we're not taught how to "own" our awesomeness, and because of this we often struggle to identify and name our strengths.

To help students "own" their awesomeness, I created the following list of characteristic traits. Look through this list and circle 4 adjectives that best describe you. Take your time doing this exercise because it's **the most important part of your entire essay-writing process.** All of your PIQ content, themes, and examples stem from these 4 attributes.

Owning Your Awesomeness

Read the List Below & Circle Your 4 Outstanding Traits

Academic Superstar
Altruistic
Artistic
Athletic
Bilingual
Bicultural
Brave
Bridge Maker
Challenge Authority
Champion for Equity
Communication Skills
Competitive Spirit
Community Organizer
Confident
Create Opportunities
Creative
Decisive
Determined
Driven
Empathetic
Environmental Activist
Feminist

Focused
Global Perspective
Goal Oriented
Grateful
Growth Mindset
Health Conscious
Honest
Humane
Humanist
Humorous
Hustler
Imaginative
Innovative
Insightful
Integrity
Intellectual Curiosity
Interpersonal Skills
Inventive
Kind
Leader
Musical
Optimistic

Organized
Original
Patient
Politically Astute
Problem Solver
Public Speaker
Reliable
Resilient
Respectful
Scientist Mindset
Scholar/Athlete
Smart
Social Justice Advocate
Spirited
Tenacious
Thoughtful
Spiritual
Trustworthy
Unique
Woke
Worldly

If you're still struggling to identify your 4 key traits, ask your peers, teachers, or parents which traits they believe you possess. Sometimes it's easier (and more obvious) for others to name these traits.

Recap

Think of your profile as 4 unique puzzle pieces.
Own your awesomeness to identify your 4 traits.
Share 4 traits the UC's *must* know about you.
Identifying your 4 traits is the most important part of this process.
Refer to list of 65 traits I've provided.
If you're stuck, have others help you identify 4 traits.

4

Step #2 - Dilo y Siguelo (Align Traits with PIQ's)

*N*ow that you've selected 4 traits, you'll need to pick 4 PIQ's aligned with those traits. How is this done? First, print a hard copy of all 8 PIQs. Grab a pen. Then, begin with your first trait. Let's say you circled "innovative" as your trait. Now look through the 8 prompts and identify which prompt is **most closely** aligned with your trait.

Using "innovative" as my trait, I looked through the list and determined PIQ #3 seemed most closely aligned with this trait: *What would you say is your greatest talent or skill? How have you developed and demonstrated that talent over time?*

I could have just as easily selected PIQ # 2: *Every person has a creative side, and it can be expressed in many ways: problem solving, original and **innovative thinking**, and artistically, to name a few. Describe how you express your creative side.* However, I like that PIQ #3 asks how I developed my talent over time. I feel I have better long-term examples to justify my decision.

I feel confident I can come up with at least 3 strong points of evidence that support my assertion. This confirms that this particular prompt easily aligns with my trait and that I'll be able to articulate several examples to showcase my awesome talent of innovativeness.

For example, I can say I used my innovative talent to help our Model UN team resolve our Yemen crisis situation. I can also say I used innovative thinking to solve a complex AP Calculus problem. Finally, I can say I used my innovative spirit to create a solution to my community's graffiti problem. Each of these examples can easily become 75-word paragraphs.

Here's another example. Let's say I selected "resilient" as my trait. I've looked through all 8 PIQ's and I know I can easily write about #4 or #5. I feel I have more examples to articulate with #5, so I'm picking that one. Now I have to pick between focusing on the educational opportunity aspect *or* overcoming an educational barrier. I'm choosing the educational opportunity aspect because I have more examples I can showcase.

I will say that because I'm a first-generation college student I had to search far and wide for programs or resources to help me prepare for the college application process. I could say that I pursued and took advantage of 3 programs. I'll talk about my participation in AVID since middle school. I'll talk about joining Upward Bound. And, I'll talk about attending the Questbridge Scholars Program. Each of these programs focuses on first generation college going students, and each are considered an "educational program." Now I know I picked the right prompt.

Super simple! You can see how easy it is to focus on your 4 traits and then find 4 prompts most aligned with those traits. I've penciled in a few more examples below, to help guide your own writing.

My Trait: Community Organizer

Aligns with PIQ: #7

My Trait: Problem Solver

Aligns with PIQ: #2

Now it's your turn. Write your 4 traits in the box below. Then, refer to your printout of the 8 PIQ's. Now, align your 4 traits with 4 PIQ's.

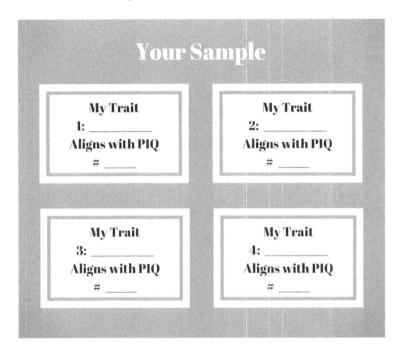

Your Sample

My Trait 1: _____
Aligns with PIQ # _____

My Trait 2: _____
Aligns with PIQ # _____

My Trait 3: _____
Aligns with PIQ # _____

My Trait 4: _____
Aligns with PIQ # _____

Check Yourself Before You Wreck Yourself

Now that you've declared your 4 amazing traits and aligned them with the PIQ's, take a quick minute to double-check your assertions versus reality. For example, let's say you listed "Social Justice Advocate" as your trait. But, you don't have any concrete evidence of your advocacy inside or outside of campus. You just wrecked yourself.

Or, if you claimed you're a Community Servant, but you've only served 12 hours of service from all 4 years of high school – then you wrecked yourself again. Double check your claims. If you're unable to provide reasonable examples or "prove" your claim, then go back to the list.

In other words, just because a prompt "feels right" or seems like an interesting prompt to write about, doesn't mean you'll have enough "evidence" to write a very compelling essay.

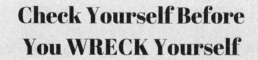

Check Yourself Before
You WRECK Yourself

 Social Justice Advocate Zero roles advocating for marginalized communities

 Community Servant Only 3 hours of community service since freshman yr

 Culturally Authentic No involvement with any cultural clubs or activities.

Recap

Align your 4 traits with PIQ's that logically match.
Select PIQ's only when you can
provide impactful examples.
Make sure you don't wreck yourself!

5

Step #3 - Los Huesos (The Bones)

So far, you've identified 4 key strengths. And, you've aligned them with a corresponding prompt. To put together a really strong essay, you'll need to do one of the most important steps in this process. You need to put together your bones (*los huesos*).

The Bones (*Los Huesos*) are simply that – the most basic and fundamental structural components of your essay. This concept forces you to sort through the gibberish and get to your main point. Forget critical analysis and eloquent sophistication. Simplicity is the key here. In fact, read what these folks says about the genius of simplicity:

> "If you can't explain it simply,
> you don't understand it well enough."
>
> — Albert Einstein

> "Life is really simple, but we insist on
> making it complicated."
> — Confucius

"Simplicity is the ultimate sophistication."
— Leonardo da Vinci

The two most important concepts of *Los Huesos* are identifying the question and answering the prompt. When the UC people designed the 8 prompts, they were obviously creating an opportunity for the majority of students to respond (aka "answer") their prompts (aka "questions"). Carefully look through each of the 8 prompts and you can see there are 8 *questions*.

These prompts may not necessarily read like a question (like, what's the answer to 1+1?), but trust me, there's a question in there. Your job is to identify the basic question and come up with the answer. The awesome thing is that there isn't an established, pre-determined answer (like 1+1 = 2). That means you'll come up with your own unique answer. Let's use PIQ #5 as an example:

PIQ #5. *Describe how you have taken advantage of a significant educational opportunity or worked to overcome an educational barrier you have faced.*

I see 2 separate questions here, separated by the conjunction "or." That means, you'll only answer one question, not both. Let's approach the first question: how you took advantage of an educational opportunity. The first thing you'll do is determine whether you indeed took advantage of an educational opportunity. You need to "check yourself before you wreck yourself" (see Chapter 4). If you're wondering what the UC people consider "educational opportunities" see Chapter 10 (Decoding the Prompts).

Let's say you participated in the COSMOS Program at UC Davis in the summer of your sophomore year. Your answer to their question is answered very simply as: *I took advantage of the educational opportunity of COSMOS.* This sentence is your THESIS. It's the answer to their question in the simplest form:

Question: Did you take advantage of an educational opportunity?

Answer: Yes, I did. The COSMOS Program at UC Davis.

You'll obviously write more (and more eloquently!), but for now, you've done the most difficult part – you've answered their question and established your thesis.

Let's look at another prompt to give you some practice. Let's take PIQ #7:

PIQ #7   *What have you done to make your school or your community a better place?*

First, identify the question. You'll need to answer their question in the simplest form:

Question: Did you make your community a better place?

Answer: Yes, I did. I founded an after-school tutoring program for English Learners at the local elementary school.

You will obviously write more, but for now, you've answered the basic question and created your thesis.

Here's another example. Let's use PIQ #3

PIQ #3: *What would you say is your greatest talent or skill? How have you developed and demonstrated that talent over time?*

The UC people are asking you 2 basic questions here. They're asking you to name your talent or skill (not both). And, they want you to elaborate on how this talent or skill evolved over time. See a list of "Talents & Skills" on the illustration, "Owning Your Awesomeness" in Chapter 3. See examples of "Talents & Skills" on the illustration following Chapter 6.

First, identify the question. You'll need to answer their question in the simplest form:

Question: What is your greatest talent or skill

Answer: My greatest talent is being a mathematician.

You will address the second half of their question in your subsequent paragraphs. But, for now you've answered the most basic question. Finally, a fourth example: PIQ #1:

PIQ #1 *Describe an example of your leadership experience in which you have positively influenced others, helped resolve disputes or contributed to group efforts over time.*

First, identify the question. The basic question is whether you've demonstrated leadership skills in some fashion. You'll need to answer to their question in the simplest form:

Question: Do you have leadership experience?

Answer: Yes, I do. I rallied a group of students to challenge a Board Policy in my school district.

It can't be that simple, right? Yes, it is. It's totally that simple. The problem is we spend way too much time worrying about whether our essay will appear clever, insightful and intellectual. We end up missing the big picture. Use this method of *Los Huesos* to simplify your writing process. It will save you time, energy, and tons of stress. Plus, it will help you nail your PIQ's.

Tip! If it's easier for you to talk versus writing your answers on paper, you can simply *talk* your way through the process. We do this in my boot camps. I break the students in pairs and they talk aloud, like this:

Marisol: What is the question asked in the prompt you selected, PIQ #1?

Javier: The question is whether I can come up with an example of my leadership experience.

Marisol: OK, so do you have an example?

Javier: Yes, my example is that I am an AVID Ambassador at my high school.

Here's another example:

Fabian: Were you able to identify the question they asked in PIQ #2?

Emilio: Yes, they are asking me to describe how I express my creative side.

Fabian: OK, so how do you express your creative side? Quetzal Mama says you should be able to tell me in one sentence.

Emilio: OK, in one sentence, here it goes. My answer is that I express my creative side through the art of rapping.

Maybe you can practice this process with a friend? Or, just speak out loud when you're in a private location. If you're like me, it might be easier to just write it down. Either way, you need to identify the fundamental question and answer it very succinctly. This means one sentence for the question and one sentence for the answer. It's not any trickier than that.

Think about this step for a moment. What you're doing is the same thing I ask my students to do in my college English Composition courses. I ask them to examine the overall content of a literary work (an essay, novel, etc.), and use critical thinking skills to identify the main point or argument. We call it an "argument" but it's the same thing you're doing here. You're identifying your point (the UC's question) and creating your argument (the thesis).

So far, you've walked through the first two steps of *Los Huesos* – identifying the question and answering the prompt. In the next chapters we'll cover the remaining 4 steps to nail your UC essays.

Recap

Simplify. Simplify. Simplify.
Use *Los Huesos* Strategy.
Read the prompt and identify the questions asked.
Answer the question(s) succinctly.
Don't overanalyze!
Your answers will become the "bones" of your essay.

6

Step #4 - Back That Thang Up! Magical Power of 3

You've carefully identified your 4 awesome traits. You've double-checked they're authentic, perfectly aligned with the contents of your application. You've used the simplified method of *Los Huesos* to identify the question asked and you've succinctly answered the question. Your answer has become your thesis.

Now comes the important part. The part where I tell you the PIQ's are like a Taco de Carne Asada. *Que?* Think of your thesis as a crispy taco shell that begs the reader to take a bite. Your UC reader wants to know more. But, what happens when your reader takes a bite of that delicious street taco and it has no *carne*? That's when you need to learn Quetzal Mama's next strategy. I call this the Magical Power of 3.

The Magical Power of 3

The Magical Power of 3 is truly magical. It's an essay writing hack that will magically transform your essay from good to extraordinary. How does it work? To explain it, let's go back to our street taco. The "*carne*" in your taco is the proof or evidence that makes your essay believable. Without it, you might as well have a taco stuffed with *lechuga y nada mas*. Your reader will go, *"Where's the carne?"* and it'll be an epic fail.

To fill up your taco, you'll need 3 credible and impactful examples. Why 3 examples? Well, for some reason, we humans prefer things in 3's. In fact, our brains are wired to want things in 3. One or two examples is not quite enough, and our brain gets overloaded with more than three examples.

I'm not the only one who's uncovered the magic of using 3's to brilliantly communicate. If you've ever watched those captivating Ted Talks, you might be surprised to know that the most successful Ted Talk presenters use the Magical Power of 3. Or, if you've ever watched some of the most successful CEO's pitch their new products or ideas, they often use the Magical Power of 3. Popular nursery rhymes, fables, and stories that have maintained popularity over the centuries have a power of 3 appeal: Three Little Pigs, Three Blind Mice, Goldilocks & the Three Bears, Three Musketeers, and on and on.

World renowned speakers throughout time have used the power of 3 in their speeches including César Chavez (Power of 3 slogan: *Si Se Puede*), Dr. Martin Luther King, Jr., President Barack Obama (*Yes we Can*), and many others.

This tool is going to be your BFF anytime you need to convince someone of something. It works when you try to win an argument with your parents. It works when you ask your teacher for extra credit. It works when applying for a job, landing a sale, or any task that involves "selling." Writing an essay IS selling. You're selling your story to the UC's. You need to convince them why they should admit you. To do this, you need to provide impactful, believable, and logical information.

Here's an example. Let's say I declare to my students that I make the best *tres leches* cake in San Diego. I can't just make the claim without any evidence. As the rapper Juvenile said, you'd better "Back That Thang Up!" To prove I make the best *tres leches* cake, I must provide evidence.

To start, if I tell them it's the most requested cake at my bakery, that's just one reference point. Meh, not so compelling. But if I add that I won my county *Tres Leches* Baking Competition, then that's another reference point. It's getting more believable. And, if I throw in one more piece of evidence and say my cake was featured on *Food Network's Cake Wars*, then I've nailed it. I just gave 3 points of evidence that backed up my claim. My taco has *carne*!

You don't need to win a Cake Wars competition on Food Network to get your point across. But, you do need to give 3 reasonable examples that back up your claim.

Below is an example of a Magical Power of 3 outline. When you write your own outline, you'll come up with three examples that back up your thesis (or claim). This is only the first step. After you've identified your three forms of "evidence" you'll begin writing expanded paragraphs of approximately 75 words each.

Magical Power of 3

PIQ #7 What have you done to make your school
or community a better place?

Community Organizer	Community Organizer	Community Organizer
I volunteered 200 hours at a women's safe house, organizing fundraisers and grassroot campaigns to advocate for women.	I founded the Neighborhood Watch Program in my neighborhood.	I was the high school representative, leading precinct walking strategies for my congressional district.

Let me share a few more examples of a Power of 3 outline using PIQ's #1, #2, and #3.

PIQ #1   Describe an example of your leadership experience in which you have positively influenced others, helped resolve disputes or contributed to group efforts over time.

I have demonstrated my leadership abilities in several contexts. First, I am the Founder of the Catholic Club. Second, I serve as our high school's Student Ambassador. Lastly, I am a member of the Student Council.

PIQ #2   Every person has a creative side, and it can be expressed in many ways: problem solving, original and innovative thinking, and artistically, to name a few. Describe how you express your creative side.

As a creative problem solver, I have utilized my creativity in several ways. First, I have used this skill to trouble shoot our Mock Trial Team's performance at the statewide competition. Second, I used creativity to conduct a provocative study on the use of capsaicin's medicinal properties. Lastly, I relied on my creativity to balance my academic workload with cross country meets and band practice.

PIQ #3 *What would you say is your greatest talent or skill? How have you developed and demonstrated that talent over time?*

My greatest talent is my ability to communicate effectively. I've developed this skill and talent over time in many different ways. First, as a mentor, I use my communication skills to speak with youth about the importance of community involvement. Second, I've enhanced my communication skills by enrolling in Communications 101 at MiraCosta College. Lastly, I have analyzed the speaking style of world renowned orators.

Now it's your turn. Use the template example above to write 3 examples that back up your claim. I know it's hard to think of examples to back it up, so I've created a list of examples to get you started. See the Illustration, *"Magical Power of 3 Examples"* in Chapter 6.

After you've identified your 3 examples to back up your thesis, you'll need your paragraphs to be as compelling and impactful as possible. To accomplish this, it's critical that you quantify and qualify your examples.

Quantify & Qualify

When writing your supporting paragraphs, you MUST show impact. To do that, you must quantify and qualify your assertion. Let's say you respond to PIQ #7 (making your community a better place). Your claim is that you indeed made your community better. You chose 3 examples to *back that thang up*. Your first evidence was stating you fundraised for a non-profit in your community. But that's not enough. You need to quantify and qualify this statement.

Instead of saying, "I fundraised for a non-profit," you can say, "Leading a team of 6, we hosted 2 donation drives each quarter, yielding $8,000 in one school year." Using language that quantifies and qualifies will help the UC people understand your level of commitment, the impact in your community, and your skills in organizing this effort.

To clearly see the difference between an impactful paragraph that quantifies and qualifies, versus a vague paragraph that lacks details, read on:

I made my community a better place. I joined the Interact Club and participated in community events, fundraisers, and recruitment. This was a fun activity and I really enjoyed it. I would do it again because I feel I made my community better off.

Versus

Throughout the last three years I have made a significant impact in my local community. As the Chairperson for Service in my campus' Interact Club, I'm in charge of recruiting students and organizing service events. In 18 months I was able to recruit 35 new students to our club, doubling the size of our membership. Increasing our membership enabled me to organize larger fundraising efforts. This resulted in a 200% increase in our fundraised profits — which led to our Club donating to three local non-profits, versus one. Overall, we fundraised $9,000, which was the largest amount raised in the history of this club.

Here's another example to illustrate the concept of quantifying and qualifying. Let's compare a lackluster and vague paragraph versus an impactful statement. We'll use PIQ #6 for this example:

PIQ #   *6:Think about an academic subject that inspires you. Describe how you have furthered this interest inside and/or outside of the classroom.*

[Lackluster & Vague]

The academic subject that inspires me is Physics. I love physics. It's challenging but it's also fun. Inside of the classroom I remain engaged and ask a lot of questions. Outside of class try to find other activities related to physics to occupy my time.

Versus

[Impactful]

As Team Captain for my high school campus' Robotics Team, I have relied on my keen knowledge of Physics theory to advance our team to the regional, state, and US Robotics competitions. My fascination with physics also compelled me to submit my entry of Dark Matter in the 2018 Breakthrough Junior Challenge where I was a finalist. Lastly, I received a perfect score of 5 on my AP Physics exam — the highest score in my school's history.

Now it's your turn. Use the template below to write in your evidence – or 3 points to back up your claim. Make sure your examples quantify and qualify your claim.

Back That Thang Up!

Trait: _____   PIQ#: _____

Evidence 1 _____

_____

_____

Evidence 2 _____

_____

_____

Evidence 3 _____

_____

_____

But it's not over yet. You can't just write one sentence explanations to back that thang up. You'll need to write three fully developed paragraphs, each paragraph about 75 words each. Using PIQ #1 as an example, your structure will look something like this:

I demonstrated my leadership abilities in three different contexts. [Introduction = @ 50-100 words]

Example 1 [_____] (75 words)

Example 2 [_____] (75 words)

Example 3 [_____] (75 words)

All of the sample essays in this book (see chapter 13) use the Magical Power of Three. Go to Chapter 13 to view how this works in a fully fleshed out 350-word essay. For an excellent list of Power of 3 examples, see the illustration on the following page.

Recap

Humans prefer things in 3.
World Leaders, TedTalk speakers, & CEO's
use Magical Power of 3.
Magical Power of 3 is just the
right amount of information.
Use 3 paragraphs to "back that thang up."
Quantify & Qualify to show impact.

Magical Power of 3 (Examples)

Academic Subject

Biology
Chemistry
Computer Science
Economics
English
Environmental Science
History
Mathematics
Physics
Psychology
World Language

Challenge/Obstacle

First Generation College Student
Fear of Public Speaking
Lack of Transportation
Mastery of Course/Subject
Homelessness
Parent(s) Incarcerated
Survivor of Abuse
Poverty
Lack of Resources
English as Second Language
Learning Disability
Gang Violence in Neighborhood
Phobia
Course (Math, Science, etc.)
Improvement in Grades
Shyness
Physical Appearance
Athletic Performance
Low-Performing School
Learning Disability
Challenge in Subject
Lack of College Advisors
Lack of Secondary Counselors
First Generation College Student
Living in Rural Area
Learning English as a Second
Language
Lacked Resources at Home
Parents Could Not Help with
Homework
No Tutors
Work Part-Time Job (Necessity)
Raised by Single Parent

Community Service

Abused Women Shelter
Beach Clean Up
Boys & Girls Club Tutor
Candy Striper
Charity Race
Church Volunteer
Coached Youth Soccer Team
Crisis hotline Volunteer
Elementary Student Tutor
Key Club Chairperson
Library Stock Shelves
Migrant Education Fair
Receptionist
Senior Center Volunteer
Service Chair for MEChA
Volunteer Homeless Shelter
Volunteer Soup Kitchen

Creative

Artistic
Chess Player
Designer
Film Director
Mathematician
Musician
Scientist
Slam Poet
Theater/Performing Arts
Videographer
Writer, Journalist

Cultural Authenticity

Community Activist
Member of MEChA
Member of Latinos Unidos
CLYLP
Ballet Folklorico Dancer
Mariachi Band
Tutor for Students of Color
Translator at Health Clinic

Greatest Talent

(See "Own Your
Awesomeness")

Educational Opp's

Academic Decathlon
Academic League
Advanced Placement
AVID
Cal Poly EPIC
CLYLP
Community College
COSMOS
edX
GEAR UP
Honors Courses
HSF Youth Leadership
MESA
Model UN
One Voice LA
Puente
Quetzal Mama Scholars
Science Olympiad
Scripps College Academy
Simon Scholars
SMASH
SMYSP
South Central Scholars
Stanford SIMR
TRIO
UCSD Triton Academy
Upward Bound
USC STAR Program

Leadership

Ambassador
Captain Sports Team
Church Choir Director
Club Officer
Designed a Program
Drum Major
Field Commander
First Chair Cellist
Founded Club
Fundraised a lot of $
Head Tutor
Lead at part-time job
Led a Protest Rally/March
Link Crew Leader
Mock Trial Lead
Oldest Sibling
Prosecutor
Social Justice Advocate

7

Step #5 - ¡Júntelo Rápido! Intro & Thesis Transition

Why is an Intro Necessary?

What would happen if you didn't have an introduction in your PIQ's? Your essay would just kind of jump out of nowhere, without a backdrop or context. Your UC reader won't know where you're going or to which point you're leading them. You've got to give them a heads up.

It's kind of like showing up at your best friend's house at 3am without texting first. She'll be like, *"Girl, what are you doing here?"* Or, like a guest speaker in your AP World History class who just walks in one day and starts talking about the spread of Buddhism in China during the post classical period. You'd scratch your head and wonder why's this dude here? Now, if your teacher introduced the speaker and told you why he was there, then you'd understand.

The same holds true for your PIQ introduction. You need to introduce your topic so your UC reader understands the context and where you're going.

Framing Your Essay

Readers need context for a thesis. Since we're working with only 350 words, you don't have enough space to slowly and strategically set the stage for your argument. However, you do need to give a little background information before jumping into your thesis. Because the typical PIQ introduction is about 50 to 100 words, you'll need to quickly introduce the topic *and* include your thesis in about 100 words or less. Below are 8 sample introductions (all @ 100 words) with **the thesis highlighted in bold**:

(Prompt #1) Last year, the Intern Coordinator from Congressmen Doug Applegate's office (49th District) came to present to our AP Government class. Something she said resonated with me deeply. She said, "If you want to see the change, you have to be the change." Her message was about "flipping" the 49th district" from Republican (and strong Trump supporter) Congressman Darryl Issa. After her speech, I decided to apply for an internship in Applegate's office. **Securing this internship enhanced my leadership skills, gave me valuable insight into positively influencing others, and most importantly – taught me how to "be the change."** (97 words)

(Prompt #2) When I was 5 years old I fell in love with the theater – the lights, costumes, music, and of course, the drama. I was determined to pursue a future in theater. However, when I arrived at my high school I realized we did not have a performing arts program (no band, choir, or musical theater). Although I was disappointed, **I knew I could rely on my creative spirit to figure out a way to champion the arts at my school.** This creativity has helped me successfully solve problems by devising creative and innovative solutions. (94 words)

(Prompt #3) I set five alarm clocks every night to ensure I get up at 3:00am. Because of the noise level in our home, I am unable to concentrate. It's not because I have problems concentrating or focusing, it's because we don't have a traditional home. My bedroom is our laundry room, and my sibling's bedroom is the garage. Therefore, I wake up early to spend quality time reading, writing, and completing assignments. I'd rather focus my energies this way, versus struggling every night with the noise of the TV. **This level of dedication to my studies – my work ethic – is my greatest talent.** (100 words)

(Prompt #4) I come from a Latinx immigrant household where my sole financial support relies on my single mother whose profession is cleaning houses. Because she was not able to further her education beyond high school in Mexico, she could not help mentor or coach me during my college preparation. It was clear to me my family's lack of financial support and overall knowledge about the college process would create significant obstacles. **Instead of dwelling on my lack of resources, I began**

searching for educational opportunities to guide me through the college process. (91 words)

(Prompt #5) During the summer of 2017, I participated in a summer academy entitled, "Grey's Anatomy" through Palomar Community College. Someone came to our academy and spoke of an exceptional internship opportunity that sparked my interest. However, when I spoke with the representative, I was heartbroken to learn that it was only available to US Citizens. This was not the only time I experienced heartbreak. It seemed every time I applied to a college-going program, an afterschool sponsored program, internship or work experience, I was disqualified. **As an undocumented student, I have faced significant challenges throughout my lifetime.** (96 words)

(Prompt #6) When I was 8 years old, I had a 4x6 whiteboard. It was as tall as me. Using this whiteboard, I would pretend to be a math teacher. I recruited my parents to be my pupils, teaching them topics I was learning in math, and even assigning homework. I taught them basic concepts like addition, subtraction, and helped them memorize multiplication tables. This was my earliest experience with **my favorite subject — mathematics.** (72 words)

(Prompt #7) I believe service to others is an obligation we all have. Looking out for each other and giving some part of ourselves to make the community better helps all of us. I've always held this conviction, and it has followed me throughout middle school and high school. In addition to the volunteer math tutoring at Mission Branch Library, and tutoring migrant education students, **I have also served in many other service capacities that have made my community a better place.** (80 words)

(Prompt #8) **The one thing that sets me apart from others is my open-minded perspective.** For example, during the summer of 2016, I completed a summer internship as an intern for a local Senator. This Senator's political platform was ideologically and politically oppositional to mine. Given the current political climate for Latino families, it was quite a challenge to remain neutral. However, I relied on my open-mindedness to overcome the situation. Rather than focusing on the negative aspects, I chose to focus on how I could learn from the experience and develop important skills. (92 words)

The above examples are essays written by my students last year. You can see they succinctly set up the context (Introduction), addressed the prompt (*Los Huesos*), and provided a smooth transition into their thesis. This strategically short intro allowed them to use the subsequent 3 paragraphs to back up their claim (Magical Power of 3). By jumping right to the answer and providing brief context, the reader can now anticipate what's to come.

Recap

No lengthy introduction.
Intro should be @ 50 to 100 words maximum.
Intro gives the context and "sets the stage."
Intro provides a smooth transition
to subsequent paragraphs.

8

Step #6 - Tu Voz (Ensure Proper Tone)

So far, you've identified your 4 awesome qualities. You've aligned these qualities with the 4 PIQ prompts that best highlight your unique background. And, you've checked yourself before you wrecked yourself. You've *backed that thang up* by providing persuasive examples using the Magical Power of 3. You quantified and qualified your examples for impact. You've incorporated an interesting (but quick!) introduction that slides right into your thesis.

All good stuff. But now it's time to check the "feel" of your essay. What kind of "feeling" am I talking about? It's a thing called *tone*.

Tone is a really cool thing. It's the result of cleverly chosen language. You can't see tone, but you can definitely *feel* it. Tone can inspire. Tone can uplift. But tone can also bring your reader down.

Think of tone as your voice. Is your voice monotone and boring? Does your voice sound bleak and pessimistic? On the other extreme, is it annoyingly positive, gushing with exaggerated enthusiasm? Or is it somewhere in the middle – inspiring, believable, and authentic? Tone is therefore, your authentic voice.

Tu Voz

The tone of your essay is directly related to how believable, persuasive, and impactful your essay will be to your readers. The tone will hit your reader's emotions. It can lead your reader to feel inspired or disappointed. Convinced or doubtful. On board or indifferent. Moving your reader to believe your story and convinced you are the student they must admit, you've got to have the right tone. Remember, you are selling something. You are selling your story. Now, before we talk about tone, I need to get out my *chancla* and warn you about taking the wrong path!

Don't be Humble. Don't Sit Down.

Yeah, it's awesome that Kendrick Lamar won a Pulitzer Prize for the album with his song, "Humble." I love Kendrick. But the concept of being humble is problematic. It's because in Latinx culture we're taught to be humble – that bragging about ourselves or our accomplishments is a trait looked down upon. That our accomplishments will stand for themselves and that if we put ourselves "out there" we'll appear self centered.

Well, that's all good for interpersonal relationships and social media. But, it's a huge mistake when it comes to crafting your UC essays. HUGE. Think about the concept I've been stressing throughout this book. I've emphasized how the essay is a sales pitch. It's selling your story. It's selling your candidacy to the University of California. If you're too humble to use assertive language to persuade and inspire, you won't make the sale.

Think about it. What if you were a car salesperson at a Honda dealership? Your customer walks onto the lot and approaches you. She's obviously interested in purchasing a Honda CRV. You tell her the Honda CRV is a *decent* car. That it's got some *basic* features. That the gas mileage is *acceptable*. Then you concede that although it's a decent car, there are other models that do an equally acceptable job – like the Toyota RAV4 or the Ford Escape.

What the heck? If your boss doesn't fire you on the spot, I'll personally drive to the lot and throw my *chancla* at you! Your job is to sell, period. You need to tell your customer the Honda CRV won the 2018 Motor Trend SUV of the year. That the CRV model has repeatedly won awards for comfort, gas mileage and affordability. That US News & World Report gave it an 8.8 out of 10 on safety, comfort, and reliability.

Did you see how I flipped that? I didn't oversell, but I certainly didn't *undersell*. You wouldn't expect a car salesperson to *undersell*, so why should you? How can you sell your story through your UC essays?

First, you've got to OWN your awesomeness. Your job isn't to be humble or concede anything. I already told you you're awesome. You wouldn't be a University of California contender without being awesome. Remember that illustration I shared in Chapter 3? You circled those traits because **they are true**. Because they represent you. Because they're authentic. Now you need to own those traits and use powerful language to convey this awesomeness to the UC people.

Second, know that using powerful language doesn't mean language that's aggressive, in-your-face, and cocky. It means using clever techniques to get to the same point without sounding like a bombastic tool. Speaking of tools, you'll need some effective tools to exert your assertive voice. To get started, I've created a list of tools that shift your voice from passive and meek, to assertive and confident.

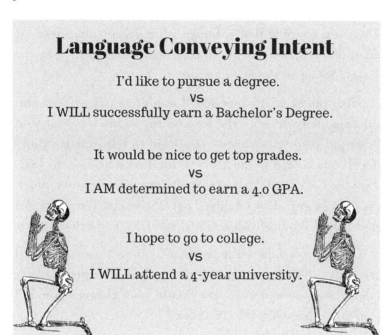

Language Conveying Intent

I'd like to pursue a degree.
VS
I WILL successfully earn a Bachelor's Degree.

It would be nice to get top grades.
VS
I AM determined to earn a 4.0 GPA.

I hope to go to college.
VS
I WILL attend a 4-year university.

You can see the language in the second sentence is more specific and intentional. Instead of leaving things to "chance" the writer is conveying full intention and determination. The reader will buy into these goals because the writer has used convincing language that conveys a specific outcome.

You can also see the writer has switched to more specific terms (e.g. Bachelors Degree versus "BA"). Technical and specific language also conveys confidence. It conveys a stronger tone. It appears the writer has researched or at least given a lot of thought to specific goals.

Don't Concede Anything!

Along the lines of being humble, many students relinquish their awesomeness. Instead of owning their gifts and talents, they concede them or use a back-handed compliment. Let me demonstrate what I mean:

 **Weak &
Conceding**

I may not be the smartest math student, but I try the hardest.

I'm lucky to be on the Academic League team.

Although I'm not the top student in AP Biology, I still enjoy it.

 **Assertive &
Convincing**

I consistently perform in the top 5% of my AP Calculus class.

I serve as the Physics expert on my campus' Academic League.

As a future genetics researcher, I am fascinated with AP Biology.

I know owning your awesomeness might make you cringe. Some of you may feel uncomfortable. Advocating assertively isn't something many of us have been taught. But think back to the Honda CRV salesperson. You've got to own your awesomeness and make the sale. There's no time to be humble. Never concede your brilliance.

Flip It!

How to Flip Your Message from Negative to Positive

The other major challenge students encounter is trying to identify and speak to a challenge or obstacle without sounding like a victim. It's really easy to fall into the "victim" voice. But that voice won't project the type of traits we need to sell your story.

The trick in selling your story is to describe a challenging situation without conveying a victim mentality. One way I help students switch out a "victim" or negative tone for a more inspirational and positive message is to *flip* the message. Flipping the message is easy when you preface your statement with the right word. Here are a few helpful words:

Powerful Words Shift Your Voice

Although	While
However	Considering
In spite of	Nevertheless

These little words are packed with power. Look at the graphic I've created for you below. Just place the adverb, "While" in front of every sentence on the left column and add a comma to the sentence. You can see how the adverb prefix and the comma link to the sentence in the right-hand column. Just adding one adverb and one comma change the entire message and tone.

Tone is also conveyed through certain topics or themes you address in your PIQ's. To learn how to avoid undesirable topics or themes that can negatively impact the tone, go to Chapter 11 (Common Mistakes).

Recap

Tone can inspire or disappoint.
Tone can convince your reader you're
the student they want.
Select language that is assertive but not overly boastful.
Flip your message from positive to
negative with my chart!
Tone is your authentic "voice."
Tone can sell your story.
Don't be humble.

Flip Negative to Positive
6 Ways to *Avoid* a "Bummer" Essay

Before (Negative Spin)	After (Positive Spin)

First Generation College Student
"No one in my family has gone to college."
"I don't have help. I'm lost."
"My struggles are overwhelming."
"My parents don't get it."

First Generation College Student
"I have an opportunity to be first."
"I have overcome challenges."
"I'm determined to make my family proud."
"My parents fully support me."

Low-Income
"I can't afford college."
"College will be a burden on my family."
"I didn't have resources like rich people."
"Being poor has closed doors."

Low-Income
"I learned how to be innovative."
"I learned to do a lot with a little."
"College will help prepare me for a career."
"My status has inspired me."

Low-Resourced High School
"My school has no resources to help me."
"We have 2 AP classes at my high school."
"The counselors don't care about us."
"We are on our own."
"I wish I was at a better school."

Low-Resourced High School
"I've identified external resources for help."
"I've taken every rigorous course available."
"Our counselors are overworked. Therefore,
I've sought help from non-traditional
sources and programs."

Being Latino
"Everyone has low expectations of me."
"People think low of my culture."
"Our teachers are racist."

Being Latino
"I'm proud of my heritage and background."
"I will bring a unique perspective."
"My cultural is an asset."

English Language Learner
"I've struggled to learn English."
"I hated being pulled out of class."
"I've wasted so much time trying to learn."

English Language Learner
"I am bi-cultural and bilingual."
"My linguistic strength has helped me."
"I can think and speak in two languages."

Extenuating Circumstances
"My life circumstances are overwhelming."
"No one understands me."
"I've had more burdens than anyone else."
"It's not fair that I had so many road blocks."

Extenuating Circumstances
"I've leaped over road blocks."
"My circumstances won't dictate my future."
"I developed valuable skills
to overcome obstacles."

9

Step #7 - ¿Y Que? Wrap Up Conclusion

You're almost there! You've crafted a compelling introduction that glided right into your strong thesis. Your thesis answered the prompt using the strategy of *Los Huesos*. You've backed up your claim using the *Magical Power of Three*. You strategically used impactful statements to back up those claims. You've used careful language to modify your tone and own your awesomeness. Now we're near the end. Our final step is to conclude our essay with an impactful paragraph. We call this paragraph the *conclusion*.

But, hold up. We're not doing the traditional, "In conclusion . . ." closing paragraph. Instead, we're summing up our points by relating this back to the UC's. After all, this whole essay writing process is 100% related to your candidacy at the University of California.

In this final step you'll round out your essay by telling the UC people, "*¿y que?*" In other words, so what (*¿y que?*) you won 1st place in a robotics competition. So what you served 250 hours of community service painting murals in Chicano Park? So what you did a summer internship at Kaiser Permanente? Why should the UC people care?

¡Eso!

In this important closing paragraph, you'll need to convince the UC people why they should care. Here is when you relate back to those 4 qualities you initially selected in Chapter 3. What do these traits have to do with your candidacy as a future UC undergraduate?

In all 4 essays you need to bring it home. Your goal is to link your argument to the larger matter of fit for college. For example, if you identified as a community servant (and responded to PIQ Prompt #7), then you need to answer the question, *y que*? So what you're a community servant? You have to tell them why they should care. And, if you follow my rubric below, you can see you must do this in about 50 words or less.

Quetzal Mama's PIQ Rubric

I. Short Intro with Thesis
   Los Huesos (@ 50-100 words)

II. Back That Thang Up
   Magical Power of 3

   Paragraph 1 (@ 75 words)
   Paragraph 2 (@ 75 words)
   Paragraph 3 (@ 75 words)

III. ¿Y Qué? Conclusion paragraph relating
   to your UC candidacy (@ 50 words)

The following are 4 examples of conclusion paragraphs from students who applied and received admission to the University of California last year. Each conclusion paragraph is @ 50 to 60 words.

Here's a student responding to PIQ Prompt #3:

Lastly, as an undocumented student I've refused to let my status hinder my future college goals. Instead, I've focused my energies and resources toward preparing myself to be as competitive, prepared, and knowledgeable in my field of astrophysics. This is the same energy and vision that will help me thrive at the University of California. (54 words)

An example responding to PIQ #4:

Each educational opportunity provided specific knowledge and unique experiences that helped me navigate the college application process. I met other students who, just like me, had a steep learning curve when it came to college admissions. Moreover, we learned psychological strategies concerning underrepresented students in higher education. I am confident these experiences prepared me mentally and psychologically for a successful transition to the University of California. (66 words)

Responding to PIQ Prompt #5:

Having overcome these obstacles, I learned being patient is critical to achieving long-term goals. Secondly, I learned to believe in myself to become a confident writer. Lastly, I learned to ask for help and develop a network of resources. I will rely on my patience, confidence, and ability to seek resources as an incoming student at the University of California. (60 words)

Lastly, an example responding to PIQ #7:

Serving 300 hours of service taught me three things. It taught me excellent time management skills. It gave me a new perspective regarding drug addiction and rehabilitation. And finally, it proved to me that one student could impact long-term success within a marginalized community. I will bring my time management skills, unique perspective, and altruistic spirit to my future University of California campus. (63 words)

When you craft your conclusion paragraph, remember you are restating what you claimed (your thesis), but not repeating your original statements. Instead, restate how the experiences or opportunities benefited you. Tell them how it impacted you in some way. And, relate it to your UC applicant candidacy.

Bottom Line

You need to convince the UC people you have the skills, resources, and talents to *thrive* at their institution. These skills, resources or talents should be directly related to your future success as a University of California undergraduate.

Recap

Use this paragraph to reemphasize your
stated quality or trait.
Explain how the experience or event shaped you.
Relate the quality or trait to your candidacy.
Remind them why they should admit you.
Complete the final paragraph in @ 50-60 words.

10

Decoding the Prompts

By now, you're very familiar with all 8 of the PIQ's. Yes, you've carefully read each prompt, but you haven't read it through the lens of a college admission consultant. You're in luck! I'm going to help you decode the prompts from an admissions perspective. In this section, I'll let you know what the UC's are asking and then I'll translate this to "high school speak." Meaning, we'll break down official UC lingo to help you understand the essence of what they're *really* looking for in your essays.

PIQ #1 *Describe an example of your leadership experience in which you have positively influenced others, helped resolve disputes or contributed to group efforts over time.*

Broken Down – First, they're giving you the big hint you don't have to be President of your ASB to earn the distinction of "leader." In other words, they don't want you to stress about an official title. They're saying if you "influenced" others or "resolved" problems, then that constitutes *leadership* for them. The other important point is that demonstrating leadership is not necessarily limited to a lone individual. You can be a leader and be part of a 3-person team. For example, were you part of a task force at your campus that dealt with bullying or discrimination?

Second, although not specifically stated in the prompt, the UC people provide additional instruction on their admissions page: "... *your leadership role doesn't necessarily have to be limited to school activities.*" That's important! This tells you that leadership can happen anywhere and in *many contexts* – including outside of your high school campus. That means you can be the eldest sibling in your home and serve as a leader (think role model) for your younger siblings. It means you can lead a group of students at your church through a year-long Confirmation process, and that's leadership. Or, you can do like my son Emilio did (current 10th grader) and demonstrate leadership by serving as part of a 6-person mentorship *team* for elementary school students.

Lastly, they're also making the point about contributing to group efforts "over time." What they're signaling here is that a one-day activity, event, or experience does not make a leader. They want to see this trait demonstrated over time. So, pick leadership examples that demonstrate a long-term commitment or where you made a significant contribution.

The Bottom Line – It's important to know that your official title or role is not what's important to the UC people. They're more interested in what you learned from your leadership experience(s) and the initiative you displayed. Did you gain important skills? Did the experience influence how you approach challenges or problems? Was your perspective about people or situations changed? Did you grow from the experience?

They also want to know how you deal with others in a group setting. Are you a great collaborator? Can you inspire others to complete the task or resolve the issue? Are you diplomatic and politically savvy in the way you assert authority? Can you handle crisis, or do you flop when you're placed in a leadership role?

Tip: While you may want to talk about your team's efforts, always remember the UC's are most interested in *you*. Make sure you bring it home and describe *your* role and *your* abilities in leading others.

PIQ #2 *Every person has a creative side, and it can be expressed in many ways: problem solving, original and innovative thinking, and artistically, to name a few. Describe how you express your creative side.*

Broken Down – Very, very few of my students pick this prompt. Why? Probably because they mistakenly associate "creativity" exclusively with the arts. They believe only sculptors, writers, musicians or theater majors can speak to this prompt.

Take a closer look. First, they're straight out telling you creativity is not limited to students pursuing fine arts! While they specifically mention expressing your creative side "artistically," they want you to know it's not limited to artistic folks. They're literally saying creativity can be "expressed in many ways."

They're telling you creativity can be expressed through the way your mind works. They align "creativity" as being synonymous with "innovative thinking." Do you use your creativity to solve complex problems? For example, mathematicians use creativity to solve complex math problems. Computer Science majors use creativity to write code. Do you successfully navigate challenges through innovating thinking? This is what they're looking for.

They're also telling you creativity can be inside or *outside* of the classroom. That means you can describe your weekend participation in a film program. Or, you can describe how you creatively choreograph waltzes for *Quinceañeras*. Or, how you use your creativity and innovative spirit to create a wonderful *flan* (think food science).

Bottom Line – they're not so interested in the actual talent. What they want you to describe is *how you use that talent* toward successful outcomes. They are curious as to how you go about approaching obstacles, and how you creatively and innovatively resolve an obstacle. They want to know how you *creatively* work through challenges, obstacles, or projects you're passionate about.

PIQ #3 *What would you say is your greatest talent or skill? How have you developed and demonstrated that talent over time?*

Broken Down – OK, stop hyperventilating. I know you see those words "greatest talent or skill" and you're panicking. You're just not sure you have any extraordinary talents or skills. Yes, you do. You have amazing qualities or you would not have made it this far. I can tell you this is one of the most difficult parts of this process – when students are required to identify and own their awesomeness. Remember, we talked about this in Chapter 8 (T*u Voz*). And, I gave you 65 examples of talents and skills in the illustration, "Own Your Awesomeness" in Chapter 3.

First, you don't need to hold a Nobel Prize, Pulitzer Prize, Academy Award, or Grammy for your talent. And, your talent doesn't need to be featured in your school or city newspaper. The UC's are more interested in learning *how* you've used your talent to accomplish goals.

Talent can be categorized as being an awesome negotiator. It can be a person who has an open mind. It can be the way you make opportunities happen where none exists. It can literally be anything you do that has helped you navigate life.

For example, my husband frequently calls me *terca* (stubborn). I tell him, "No. I'm *tenacious,* not stubborn." After rolling my eyes, I remind him that my awesome quality of being *tenacious* has helped me overcome lots of obstacles and create amazing things (like publishing this book!). In fact, if I responded to this prompt, I'd probably say my greatest talent or skill is my tenacious spirit.

The UC's want to know how you use this talent or skill inside or outside the classroom. If your talent or skill is being a great communicator, you could identify many ways you've utilized your strong communication skills outside of the classroom. For example, are you the designated translator for your parent's doctor's appointments? Do you write for your school newspaper? Are you part of the Speech & Debate Club? Those are 3 great examples of how you've used your talent of being a great *communicator.*

Now, here's the tricky part. Although you'll obviously need to be assertive and claim your awesomeness, you'll also need to keep a level head. Meaning, you don't want to come across like you're full of yourself or superior to others. How can you walk this tightrope?

Step into my classroom. Let me share a secret tip I share with my students. The secret is to think of your awesome trait, skill, talent, etc., as an accomplishment or triumph over an adversity. Meaning, you won't just list all of your talents – as if you're bragging. Instead, you'll describe a "win" or triumph that resulted from the use of your awesome trait, skill, talent, etc. For example, consider this boastful statement:

> "*I am a brilliant speaker. My talent is my presentation skills. My brilliant presentation skills led to winning Best Defense Attorney in our county's Mock Trial competition.*"

That doesn't sound appealing, does it? Now, read the following sentences that showcase the same talent, but places emphasis on the triumph over adversity. It also conveys a spirit of gratitude:

> "*Prior to the competition, I spent more than 100 hours practicing speech strategies and tactics. I watched TedX videos, read the book, "Talk Like Ted" and rehearsed with my team. This effort helped me develop my greatest talent – my presentation skills. I'm grateful to have put in the effort that led to receiving the Best Defense Attorney award at our County Mock Trial Competition.*"

In both scenarios, the writer names the awesome trait. But, writer #1 places emphasis on possessing the talent. Whereas, writer #2 focuses on *how* she used the talent to accomplish a goal. She describes how hard work led to her superior presentation skills. The focus is on the triumph, and her wonderful presentation skills are secondary. She still got her point across, but successfully avoided the trap of sounding arrogant. Nailed it.

Bottom Line – The UC's want you to name the talent or skill and tell them why it's important to you. You'll need to give examples of how you have positively utilized this talent or skill. This talent or skill can be demonstrated inside or outside of the classroom. Lastly, you need to OWN your awesomeness. But don't forget to use my secret tip to avoid sounding arrogant.

PIQ #4 Describe how you have taken advantage of a significant educational opportunity or worked to overcome an educational barrier you have faced.

Broken Down – Be careful with this prompt. This is the only PIQ that includes 2 different options in the same prompt. In other words, there are 2 different questions here. You will NOT respond to both questions. You will respond to one *or* the other. Not both. We'll start with the first option.

The first option asks you to talk about an educational opportunity. The UC's are intentionally very broad with this prompt. They tell you this opportunity can be ". . . *anything that has added value to your educational experience and better prepared you for college.*" I make every one of my students write about this prompt! It's because, by default of participating in my Quetzal Mama Scholars Program or my UC Boot Camps, they took advantage of an educational program. There are tons of educational programs. For a full list of examples, see Chapter 6 (Magical Power of 3 Examples).

If you choose to speak about an educational opportunity, you're basically going to do three things. First, you'll name the opportunity. Tell them the name of the program and give some context. Don't use acronyms! The UC readers may not know what SHPE or SACNAS stands for, so spell it out. Second, you'll describe *how* you took advantage of this opportunity. What did it do for you? What skills or strategies did you yield from this opportunity? Give specifics. Lastly, you'll describe the outcome. By participating in this program and learning new skills, what did it ultimately yield?

The second option focuses on an educational barrier you've faced. What do they mean? They're referring to any obstacle or challenge you encountered along your educational path. It could be learning English as a second language. It could be overcoming a math phobia. Being an undocumented student is an educational barrier. Attending very low performing schools is an educational barrier. If your high school only has 1 counselor for 3,500 students, that's a huge obstacle. If you need more examples, see the Illustration, "*Magical Power of 3 Examples*" in Chapter 6.

Bottom Line – With both of these options, the UC people are not so concerned about the actual educational program or the academic barrier. What they really want to know is *how* you took advantage of the educational program to advance your future success. *How* did your participation help you become successful? We'll talk more about obstacles and challenges in the next prompt.

PIQ #5 *Describe the most significant challenge you have faced and the steps you have taken to overcome this challenge. How has this challenge affected your academic achievement?*

While PIQ #3 is the hardest prompt for my students, PIQ #5 is the easiest and most popular. It's easy because the majority of students I've coached have faced incredible challenges. Many of my students live below poverty level, are undocumented, foster youth, homeless, have a parent incarcerated, or are first in their family to attend college. Most do not have the college-going capital in their communities to navigate the complex college admission process. These are all significant challenges.

Broken Down – Pay attention because this prompt requires you to answer 3 things. They want you to first identify the challenge. Then, they want you to describe the steps you took to overcome the challenge. Lastly, they want you to tell them *how* the challenge affected your academic achievement. That means you've got to cover all 3 of these points in your 350-word essay. And, they want you to focus on your *academic achievement*.

Bottom Line – It's not enough to simply tell them about the challenge. In other words, don't use all 350 words to focus on describing the challenge. They want you to specifically address what you're doing (or what you've done) to overcome the challenge. Did you navigate the challenge by yourself or did you have help? What resources did you utilize? Lastly, what did you *learn* from this experience?

I hope you're starting to see the trend now – that the UC's are not so concerned with the talent, obstacle, or opportunity you list. What they really want is for you to tell them *what* you did with that skill or talent and *how* you navigated through the obstacle.

The UC's value resourcefulness, resilience, and tenacity. You can describe these traits via the topics you choose to write about. Describing how you utilized your strengths and resources successfully can inform them how you might be successful at their campus.

Tip: Be careful with this prompt. This is not an opportunity to tell the UC's about all of your faults. Whichever challenge you identify, you'll need to describe how you overcame it and were ultimately successful. And, you'll need to tie this wonderful ability to how it may serve you as an undergraduate at one of their campuses.

To help you work through this prompt, I've compiled a full list of "Significant Challenges." See Chapter 6 (Magical Power of 3 Examples).

PIQ #6 *Think about an academic subject that inspires you. Describe how you have furthered this interest inside and/or outside of the classroom.*

Broken Down – The very first line in the prompt flat out tells you to focus on an *academic subject*. That means don't talk about your dance class, band, PE, or some other non-academic topic. The following is a sample list of academic subjects (not an exhaustive list):

Biology

Chemistry

Computer Science

Economics
English
Environmental Science
History
Mathematics
Physics
Psychology
World Language

Next, you'll need to pick a subject where you can demonstrate superior performance! Duh. For example, you wouldn't pick AP Physics if you got a D in both semesters. Finally, pick a subject where you can write at least a few examples of how you furthered your interest inside and/or outside of the classroom.

For example, if you claim to be passionate about STEM, can you adequately share examples related to this passion? Examples might be receiving A grades in AP Bio, AP Calculus, and AP Chemistry. Or, doing a summer internship at the Stanford Medical Youth Science Program. Or, volunteering for *Los Medicos Voladores*. President of the Pre-Med Club at your high school? Did you attend COSMOS? Do you read books about Human Biology in your spare time?

Lastly, you'll tie this together with your intended major and career goals. For example, if you state your passion is Biological Sciences, is this aligned with your goals to major in Human Biology or Molecular & Cell Biology? Do you intend to be a future physician? Make sure you connect your interest in the academic subject with your future academic and career goals.

Quetzal Mama's Insider Tip!

In my 2-day UC Essay Writing Boot Camp, I encourage every student to consider writing about PIQ #6. I also insist all of my Quetzal Mama Scholars write about PIQ #6. Why should you care about PIQ #6? Because it's the only prompt that specifically addresses an academic subject. Meaning, it's the prompt that lets you showcase your talents and fit for your **declared major** in your UC application. Remember, you are applying to both the UC campus and the major at the campus. This prompt helps you hone in your specific abilities, accomplishments, and talents directly related to your future major.

Bottom Line – It's got to be an academic subject. You need to have reasonable evidence to prove your passion for this subject. Your passion can be demonstrated inside or outside the classroom. Lastly, how did your participation or pursuit of this subject influence or impact your decision to pursue this major at the UC's and/or your future career goals?

PIQ #7 *What have you done to make your school or your community a better place?*

Broken Down – The UC's use the term, "community" loosely. They say it can be your team, workplace, on-campus club, service organization, or your hometown. In other words, it's not necessarily limited to traditional "community service." This means it could be your faith community. Or, the LGBTQ community. Or, the immigrant rights community.

Why do think colleges are interested in students who care about their community? It's because students who serve selflessly (we call this *"altruism"*) tend to possess a very unique mindset. These students believe their actions can actually impact change on a broader scale. More than likely, these types of students will go on to create wonderful change and impact their future communities – at their undergraduate campus, within the political arena, international affairs, or in their respective fields.

Bottom Line – They want to know your role in improving your community. What did you do? What drove you to serve? How did you solve a problem? After identifying your role, you need to explain what inspired you. How did you get it done? What was the outcome or impact? Ultimately, how did your involvement make your community a better place? For a list of Community Service examples, see Chapter 6 (Magical Power of 3 Examples).

PIQ #8 *Beyond what has already been shared in your application, what do you believe makes you stand out as a strong candidate for admissions to the University of California?*

Broken Down – I'd estimate less than 5% of students I've coached have selected this prompt. It's because the majority of students will be able to identify with most of the other 7 prompts. However, my students who used this prompt did so because they felt they had more than 1 extraordinary talent or gift to describe. They already wrote a 350-word essay responding to PIQ #3 (Greatest Talent or Skill), but still felt they have another compelling trait they wanted to speak about. This prompt provides the perfect avenue do to so.

You'll also see that none of the other 7 PIQ's address diversity, inclusion, or cultural authenticity. Many of my students use this prompt to speak to their unique racial/ethnic or cultural background. You can see two excellent examples of Prompt #8 in Chapter 13.

But, they're not giving you a free-for-all! You can't simply talk about any subject. For example, you wouldn't use this prompt to tell them *chiles en nogada* is your favorite meal. There are boundaries. They want you to focus on how you stand out as a candidate for admission to the University of California.

Bottom Line – Use this prompt only if you can address a powerful skill, talent, ability or topic that *wasn't already covered* in the previous prompts. In other words, don't make the mistake of *The Broken Record Essay* (see Chapter 11).

Now that you've read my brief discussions following each prompt, hopefully you've identified a pattern. The UC's want to know what's important to you. They want to know what you're passionate about. They want to know how you approach stuff. How you navigate situations. And they want to know this in the context of your academic journey.

Recap

There is a specific strategy for each prompt.
Understand "UC Speak" by decoding the prompts above.
Notice the pattern in each decoded prompt.
Once you identify the patterns, you'll nail your essays!

11

The Most Common Mistakes (aka Do NOT Do This)

There are seriously lots of mistakes students make each year when writing their PIQ's. But, here's some very common mistakes many students make. I'm sharing the top 10 mistakes below so you avoid them.

The Homage to Abuela Concha or Tia Yolanda (or Mamá y Papá)

The essay is about you, period. When students use 250 of their 350 word-count to talk about their awesome *abuela* (because all *abuelas* are awesome), they lose focus of what the UC people want. They want to know about YOU. Sure, Tia Yolanda might make a killer *torta*, but unless you used her recipe to build a 4.3M *torta* empire, it's really insignificant. Focus on you. If your *abuela* introduced you to her *hierbera* skills, and that introduction compelled you to study Plant Biology, then say that! If abuela introduced you to Oaxacan cuisine and you intend to study Food Science, say that. But, limit the reference to a few sentences. Then go on to talk about YOU.

Ditto on your parents. Referencing your *mamá or papa* is totally fine. Just don't spend half of your essay talking about how your parents influenced you to pursue a 4-year degree. You can reference their influence and set the context within one paragraph. Then, use the rest of the essay to talk about YOU. Remember, your introductory paragraph will likely be @ 75 words. Your introduction should include your thesis (or at least lead the reader toward your thesis).

El Ensayo de Venganza
The Revenge Essay

Before I talk about this particular theme, I want you to know I'm not trivializing or poking fun here. When students present me with a "revenge" essay, I respect and understand the power in speaking this truth. I've been told far too many times by too many students, about being told by a teacher, counselor, via mass media stereotypes, or by a person of authority, that they won't succeed. That they're not smart. That they're not "college material." That "All Mexicans are dumb." Or, hang on, "Don't waste your time applying to the UC's".

So, when I see students using 350 precious words to "get back" or address these serious issues, I tell them this: "Don't give them a single word." While a teacher's negative comment in 3rd grade might have inspired you to "prove them wrong," I don't believe for a moment you're an incredible scholar *because of them*. This is all you. You got here because of your intelligence, traits, driven nature, and resilience. Tell the UC's about that. Don't waste valuable space saying you're going to "show them all."

More importantly, think about how your reader will assess this type of essay? Is it smart or strategic for a student to spend an entire essay speaking about getting revenge on someone who hurt their feelings or crushed their ego? No, it won't. Instead, that student will come across as very shallow, fragile, and vindictive. That's not what the UC's want! The UC's want students who can handle stress, adversity, and other challenges that life throws at us. Bottom line – don't waste 350 words on a negative topic.

The Creative Writing Experiment

If you begin your essay with, "Do we truly have free will?" or "What is the meaning of God?" Or, "What is true happiness?" Stop. You're heading in the wrong direction. Using the PIQ's to address philosophical questions is a bad idea.

Likewise, if you're thinking about rapping your UC prompt to show them how creative you are, think again. And don't even think about writing a stream of consciousness because you're a "deep thinker." Slam poetry, haiku? No and no.

Also, this is not a journal entry. If you're compelled to try out some creative writing experiment, start a writing jam session with some friends at your local coffee shop. Heck, you can even write about *that* in your PIQ!

The TMI Essay
(Too Much Information)

It's baffling to me that students who would otherwise *never* share traumatic, personal experiences with friends, family, or on social media, somehow feel it's the right time and place to share in their UC essays. I imagine the writing process might trigger certain memories or traumas, and because of this, students become inclined to write about extremely personal experiences.

The reality is there are simply some topics that are a no-no when writing your PIQ's. It's because (a) you don't have enough space to provide adequate context; (b) you need to focus on your positive traits and wonderful qualities; (c) unless you're an extraordinarily gifted writer, it's going to be hit or miss.

What are examples of inappropriate topics? Here's a few: mental illness, victim of sexual abuse, an abortion, your sex life, criminal involvement, doing drugs, cheating in school, or anything that would compromise your candidacy.

What I tell students about "touchy" topics is this: "Does it pass the *abuela* test?" Meaning, would you feel comfortable with *abuela* reading your essay? If it's not appropriate for *abuela*, then it's definitely not appropriate for the UC people!

Now, there's an exception to this rule. The exception is when that sensitive personal situation or experience *positively* impacted the student. For example, if the student was a victim of physical abuse and that experience influenced their decision to pursue a career in Child Psychology (and declare Psychology as their major), then yeah. Or, if the student suffered from mental illness and received medication that turned their life around, then it might be appropriate to discuss.

Bottom line? My professional opinion is to avoid these touchy topics because it's better to be safe than sorry. It's better to play it safe and write 4 extraordinary essays, versus taking a risk and possibly jeopardizing your shot at a UC.

The White Flag Essay
(Defeated Before the Game's Begun!)

This essay is named, "The White Flag" because it's written in a concessionary way that signals defeat even before the game's begun. In this case, the game is college and the player is the student. The student writes about historic oppression and how Latinx students experience extraordinary hurdles in their path to college. Yes, this is absolutely factual and a reality for many Latinx students. However, this essay is problematic for three reasons.

First, when students use 350 words to describe oppression, racism, and other obstacles, it doesn't tell the UC people anything about the student. Again, while this is a factual claim, being self-righteous won't score you any points.

Second, these essays tend to have language and a particular tone that signals victimization. Worse, it signals that the student has already conceded they will be another casualty in this game called college. That's not our goal. We want to project a winner mentality and spirit.

Lastly, this type of essay puts the reader on the defensive. After all, we're calling out institutional racism and practices that harm Latinx students. The UC's are an institution. We have plenty of time to voice our opinion as an undergraduate student! The game is getting admission to your desired campus – not offending or alienating our readers. See the "Playing the Victim" description below.

Que Asco
(The Ewww Yuck Essay)

Sometimes students get a little carried away by providing too many descriptive details. They write about pus oozing out of open sores to describe their interest in dermatology. Or, they talk about vomiting purple chunks to describe their fascination with the human digestive system. How about describing an itchy burning sensation of Athlete's Foot? Gross. Don't do this.

You can easily find other ways to describe an interesting story or to put things in context. The problem is your reader will focus and remember the titillating details (and grossness) instead of being inspired by your story. You're creative – find some other examples or word choices to convey your points.

Playing the Victim
(The *Womp Womp* Essay)

I'm the first one to persuade students to share any adversities or hardships they encountered in their trajectory to college. But, it's not to make the UC reader feel sorry for you. It's to *showcase* your incredible talents in **overcoming** the challenge.

The point is not to focus on the particular challenge – using most of your word count to describe this challenge. Mention the challenge but focus on what you did to overcome that challenge. It's the overcoming part that's of interest to the UC people.

They want to know what you did, how you responded, what resources you used, what strategies you employed, and what personal characteristics you drew from to overcome the obstacle. Bottom line – they want you to be successful at their UC campus as much as you want to be successful.

Remember, the University of California is a world-renowned institution. They admit some of the top minds and brightest students in the world. They know their curriculum is rigorous, and that students will be challenged. For that reason, they're looking for students who have the skills, strategies, and wherewithal to navigate future challenges.

In other words, if you encounter any challenges as a UC student, they want to know you're equipped to deal with it. For that reason, it's fine to share some of your hardships and obstacles. Just make sure you give examples of how you successfully maneuvered through those obstacles.

I'm Down with the Brown
The Cultural Incompetence Essay

If you're attempting to show the UC's you're "down with the brown" you'd better check yourself. Many students become "ethnic" in their senior year of high school falsely believing this newfound identity might be a hook for admission. They've never embraced their racial or ethnic heritage and have no affiliation with any cultural or ethnic groups like MEChA or the Chicanx Club. Then, all of a sudden they want to write essays about their love of *huitlacoche* and *Los Tigres del Norte*. Come on. #Fake.

Some of the telltale signs of the culturally incompetent writers are the improper use of political terms. For example, I've seen countless essays where students claim they're proud to be "Latin" or "Spanish." Their incompetence evades their knowledge of the most basic facts. Latin is an Italic language spoken in ancient Rome, referring to a native of Latium (and ancient Roman). It is not short for "Latino." Spanish refers to Spanish people (who are European, not Latinx!) or the Romance language of Spain. Spanish is not a term to reference Latinxs.

Don't make the mistake of trying to play up your "ethnicity" if you don't have an authentic story to tell. It will be obvious to the reader – if not from your essay, then definitely from your populated application.

¡Qué Chistoso!
The Humorous Essay

Unless you've been gifted with the humor gene like Gabriel "Fluffy" Iglesias, leave your standup comic mic at home. Trying to be funny *and* respectful is tricky. Plus, humor often comes across as cheesy. And, it could come across as disrespectful. So, avoid the humor. No jokes. No one-liners. Enough said.

The Broken Record Essay
Otravez?

When you're working on the Puzzle Strategy I shared in Chapter 3, you are coming up with FOUR characteristic traits. Let me repeat, that's four different traits. Sometimes students will mistakenly use the same trait, skill, or quality, and reference it in all four essays.

It goes like this. In the first essay they'll say their greatest strength is their skill in *mathematics*. Then, in their second essay they'll say they provide community service by tutoring students in *mathematics*. In their third essay they'll talk about their favorite academic subject – guess what? Yep, *mathematics*.

And lastly, in their fourth essay they'll talk about how they use their creativity to solve *mathematic* problems.

So, while these are technically different essays, all four essays focus on the same quality (mathematics). It's repetitive and doesn't allow you to showcase your other compelling traits or talents. And, it's boring. Bottom line – don't be a broken record. Make sure each of your four essays highlights a unique talent, trait, or skill.

Other Mistakes

So far, these examples have related to tone, content, language or theme. I want to share a few additional examples that have to do with the mechanics of writing college essays. Here's a quick list of common mistakes and examples so you can "see" what I'm talking about.

Pile of Loose Puzzle Pieces

When I see an essay that's one long, continuous paragraph, it's a red flag. It signals the writer had difficulty organizing their thoughts (and subsequently, organizing their paragraphs). It gives the impression everything is just piled on haphazardly – like the writer just threw together a whole bunch of words. What does this look like? Here's a sample:

Big Pile of Puzzle Pieces

My dad didn't really want me to go to college. But I struggled to be a good student and I wanted to be the first in my family so I worked really hard and pushed myself to be the best I could be. My cousin went to college and so did my neighbor's son. They're good students too. My friends all talk about college and how fun it will be. We walk together and talk about college. When I'm in my AVID class we talk about college too and there's lots of students who also want to be first in their families to go to college. I've been researching colleges like Stanford and Harvard and I really like their architecture. Plus the name is really well known. That's another reason I want to go to college so I can do sports and get involved in the community. I pretty much took the right classes to be prepared. That's for sure.

In this example, it's difficult to decipher the thesis. I can't identify the main point the writer is trying to express. It's also a red flag to the UC readers because it signals the student struggles to follow directions, devise a cohesive argument, and write at the level they seek. Even worse: it signals the writer may not have critical thinking skills. We don't want that. If your essay does not follow a logical structure, review your essay against Quetzal Mama's 7 steps.

Not Answering the Prompt
Staying In Your Lane

When students sit down to contemplate an essay, they often get thrown off track. Instead of using the tools I shared in Chapter 5 (*Los Huesos*), they forget to answer the prompt. They go off into different directions – often in tangents unrelated to their basic thesis. I try to steer them back to the original question (or prompt) asked by the UC people. I tell them, *"If I cannot identify your thesis, neither will the UC readers."* Here is an example of a student going off into another direction and not answering the prompt.

> When I wake up in the morning the first thing I do is flick the light switch to turn on my Krups coffee maker. I need a lot of energy in the morning so I program a cup ready to go each day. I get my clothes ready and start packing my backpack for my long walk to school. Once at school I will start my day in my favorite class: AP English. Mr. Gonzalez is my favorite teacher and he makes the class fun. This year we're reading some interesting books like *Pride & Prejudice* and *Wuthering Heights*. This class is fun, but not as fun as AP World History. In this class we're studying so many interesting facts about history. I've focused a lot in preparing for these classes, so I haven't really had time to focus on extracurricular activities.

Hmm. Try to guess which prompt our student is responding to? Is it clear? Does she answer it succinctly? Or, is it a mystery? It's a mystery because we have no idea which PIQ she chose. Is she talking about a significant challenge (PIQ #5)? Or, is it the favorite academic subject (PIQ#6)? Who knows? We have no idea because she has not clearly stated her thesis. You'll need to succinctly answer the prompt and make it very clear.

Recap

Avoid common mistakes.

Language is critical – select appropriate language.

The PIQ's are not a journal writing exercise.

Don't attempt humor, colloquialisms,

or over the top language.

When in doubt, follow the *Abuela Rule*.

12

¿Y Es Todo? Anything Else You Want to Tell Us?

There is a section at the very end of your UC application that asks if there is "anything else" you'd like to tell the UC people. You're probably wondering what on earth the UC people need to know about you that hasn't already been addressed in your application and essays?

The majority of my students will not write the "anything else" essay. It's because they've successfully captured their unique obstacles and challenges in their PIQ's. Also, because after reading the instructions, they quickly understand this isn't an extension of a PIQ:

"Use this space to explain unusual circumstances, not as an extension of a personal insight question response."

But, there are a few students each year who I recommend using that option to submit additional information. There are basically 3 reasons a student would want to take advantage of the "anything else" essay.

First Reason – The first reason is to explain something that hasn't already been covered in your PIQ's. This might be to explain something they could not discern from your essays or your application.

For example, I had a student whose mother got deported to Mexico when she was a Freshman in high school. The family moved to Mexico to be with the mom, of course. But, this move caused the student to start mathematics all over again in Mexico. Two years later when she returned to school in the US, her school placed her in a lower level mathematics track. That meant she had to start mathematics all over again. Why would the UC's care about this? Because this student was declaring mathematics as her intended major. She simply didn't have enough space to explain this unique situation in her PIQ's. She wanted the UC's to know why her mathematics courses were not aligned with someone who wanted to major in Applied Mathematics.

Second Reason – The second reason you might use the "anything else" essay would be to provide *additional* information about unique circumstances that affected your academic performance. Now, be careful here. They're not interested in hearing about ineffective teachers, disadvantageous grading policies, or that your pet cockatiel died an untimely death.

Many students ask me if writing about their parent's divorce or their best friend moving out of state qualifies as an extenuating circumstance? No, and no. However, if your parent's divorce led you to start a club at your campus for students dealing with divorce, that's different. But you'd use that example in your PIQ's, not here. Similarly, if their divorce caused you to slump into a depression that caused your grades to go from a 3.5 to a 2.0, then you might consider this.

The friend's cross-country move? Now, if your friend's cross-country move resulted in your forming a pen pal blog that has 10,000 followers? Same thing. You need to include that in your PIQ's, not in the "anything else" essay. But, if your friend's move compelled you to move across country and enroll for a year in another school district, then it could apply. That would explain why you are submitting transcripts from 2 different school districts.

Another qualifying example could be related to entrance exam scores. For example, what if you have a learning disability but are not taking medications or receiving any type of intervention or therapy. In other words, you just "winged it" on your exams? If you believe this disadvantage caused you to submit test scores that are misaligned with your talents and abilities, then you might want to tell them.

Be careful though. Don't write a statement about your less than superior SAT or ACT scores if you cannot provide evidence to explain the result. For example, you cannot simply write a statement that says, *"My test scores do not represent my abilities or intellect."* I'm sure most students could easily make this claim because they believe this to be true. Instead, you must provide evidence to back up your claim. If on the day you took the exam your sibling died, then that is a logical reason to explain your test score.

On that same note, don't use this space to present your argument that the exams are biased. I agree with you 100%, but this is just not the appropriate place to discuss your political views.

Third Reason – the third reason you might consider using the *"anything else"* essay is when you have a logical, justifiable and reasonable explanation. Many students mistakenly believe their situation qualifies for this essay. Unless you're able to provide something to "back that thang up" you'd better skip this essay. Your explanation must be aligned with a common sense, cause-and-effect rationale. Let me explain.

For example, if you say your parent's divorce caused your grades to slip, then you must be able to show a "cause-and-effect" relationship. If your parents got divorced in your senior year of high school, but you've consistently held a 2.5 GPA since your Freshman year, that's not logical or reasonable.

Now, if your parents divorced in your sophomore year, and your grade slippage coincided with your sophomore year grades (Freshman and Junior years were top grades), then that makes logical sense. It can be easily determined by a simple review of your transcript.

Similarly, what if you say your grades dropped because of a particular teacher? It was Mr. Ramirez in AP Physics. But, your transcript reflects C and D grades in other courses not taught by Mr. Ramirez. How does that make sense? Your claim is not logical.

About Ineffective Teachers: I never advise students to write about an effective teacher – regardless of how awful that teacher might have been. This statement always reads as whiny, complaining, and defensive. More importantly, it signals to the UC reader this student's default is to come up with excuses for their performance. Anyone can complain and make excuses. It's the student who figured out a way to navigate through challenges that are of greatest interest to the UC's.

How to Structure your Statement

Now that you know what qualifies (and what doesn't) for the "anything else" essay, let me share how to effectively structure your statement. It's pretty simple. While you've got a maximum of 550 characters (not words) to respond, you shouldn't need more than one short paragraph.

First, you'll state the issue and context. For example, perhaps a learning disability, a move out of the country, or a parent being deported. These are just examples. Obviously, every student is unique, so this is not an exhaustive list.

After stating the issue and context, you need to provide a reasonable and logical explanation. This explanation must be aligned with a cause-and-effect relationship. For example, if you assert you have a learning disability, but hold a 4.0 GPA, you need to explain that. You need to tell them that the teachers provided you with extra time during class, but the College Board did not give you an accommodation for your AP exams, SAT Subject Tests, SAT or ACT exams. That makes logical sense. That is aligned with your test scores and grades on your transcript.

Finally, after stating the issue, providing context and a logical explanation, you'll need to close by relating this back to your University of California candidacy. For example, if you say your test scores are low, then you need to assert that your test scores are not indicative of your intellectual abilities and talents.

In addition to the opportunity to share additional information in the PIQ section, the UC's also provide you with 550 characters to explain anything related to your academic history. This section is in the main application and can include any related issues such as:

Grades

Changing Schools

Test Scores

Units

Re-Takes

Academic Dishonesty

School Doesn't Have AP Classes

Medical or Mental Issue

Whether you are responding to the "Other Academic History" section or the end of the PIQ section, follow the above instructions to effectively state your case. Remember, you are NOT required to submit these explanations as they are reserved for extenuating circumstances.

13

Sample Essays

The following essays are examples for each of the 8 PIQ prompts. Each writer used Quetzal Mama's 7 critical steps and followed the rubric I've shared in this book. All of these essays were developed by students who attended my UC Essay Boot Camps or my Quetzal Mama Scholars Program. These students generously agreed to share their stories to help you "see" what an excellent essay looks like.

After each essay, I give commentary to help you identify the key strategies in this book and how the student used the strategies to create an awesome essay. Enjoy!

PIQ #1Describe an example of your leadership experience in which you have positively influenced others, helped resolve disputes or contributed to group efforts over time.

PIQ #1 (Leadership)

At 15, I spoke in front of a group of 30 young students at Mission San Luis Rey Church. I was teaching them about the *Gospel According to Matthew*, and how it applies to their lives. In that moment, I saw the look in their eyes, and how they were reflecting on what I was saying. I knew what I was saying was relevant to their lives, and that they were inspired to make change. I fell in love with the art of preaching and knew I needed to use my position as a leader, to continue teaching about faith and positively influencing others.

This experience has led me to many leadership roles in my community. For example, I am the Founder of my high school campus' Catholic Club. We are over 60 members, and we meet once a week to learn more about our faith and how to grow our relationship with God. It's beautiful to watch the younger classmen question and wonder about their faith, and to impact their commitment to their faith. I've also improved my communication skills and learned how to collaborate with others. I've grown in confidence, and I feel I have a purpose to preach the faith.

Outside of my leadership experience through my faith-based programs, I am also a leader at my high school campus. I am a Student Ambassador at El Camino High School. In this leadership role, I visit elementary and middle school students, and speak with them about their future high school experience. I am also third-year member of the Student Council. In this leadership role, I work with a team to design our agendas, budgets, and community service projects.

I believe my skills as a leader come from my belief that "stepping up" is the responsibility of all of us. I feel that we can all lead different people, at different times, and in different ways. I will continue to lead in the best way that I can – whether that is preaching, mentoring, or inspiring others to become their very best.

My Commentary

I shared this wonderful essay to highlight how this student's commitment to his Catholic faith is aligned with strong leadership skills. He starts off with a story that pinpoints the moment he was placed in a leadership role. He goes on to describe how that experience compelled him to form a club at his high school – where he continued to lead students. Lastly, he discusses leading students as a Student Ambassador and member of the Student Council. Did you catch how he used the Magical Power of 3 to share three examples of his leadership abilities? Finally, his clever strategy of tying together his leadership with his faith makes sense as he was applying as a Theology major. He nailed it.

PIQ#1 (Leadership)

I define myself as a collaborative leader, valuing and appreciating diverse perspectives, even when those perspectives conflict with my own. I've demonstrated this collaborative leadership in many roles and in many contexts.

I currently serve as the only female (Latina) District School Board Representative. While some board members views frequently differ from mine, I find creative ways to collaborate and build consensus. Additionally, as Youth Commissioner for the Vista Community & Safety Commission I have spoken up regarding racial division in our city, including Border Patrol checkpoints at targeted locations where Latinx communities congregate. Speaking to the Chief of Police, I voiced my perspective as a resident of the South Side of Vista. In both contexts, I have created dialogue that led to new ideas and new perspectives.

As a Girls State representative, I felt the homogeneity of our gender created a positive atmosphere that diminished inhibitions and competitiveness. Although my perspective as a "Torrey" representing the Democratic party was distinct from the "Whigs" representing the Republican party, I used my leadership skills to diffuse tension and bridge collaboration.

Outside of political and community service leadership roles, I also serve as an athletic leader. Serving as Captain of the JV water polo team, I serve as a team mentor. While sports are about competition and winning, they are also about sportsmanship and representing your school. When team members were bickering, disagreeing, or having an off day, I would remind them that each of us plays a critical role and we all win together.

Lastly, as Founder and President of our campus' chapter of Movimiento Estudiantil ChicanX de Aztlán (MEChA), I advocate for political empowerment by speaking about policies and practices that impact our community. Working with a team of officers, we collaborate and build consensus so that our club can benefit from multiple perspectives and experiences.

Whether leading as a School Board Representative, Youth Commissioner, Captain of the JV Water Polo Team, as a Girls State Representative, or empowering students in MEChA, I use my leadership ability to bridge differences and ultimately create positive change.

My Commentary

This essay works because she starts off defining her leadership style as one who values and respects the perspectives of others. She then provides clear examples of how she utilized her leadership talent in different contexts. She walks us through the unique leadership roles she held in her district, community, sports team, and on-campus club. In each example, she consistently refers back to how her leadership style led her to a successful outcome. There's a "win" at the end of each paragraph, emphasizing her success. She nailed it!

PIQ #2   Every person has a creative side, and it can be expressed in many ways: problem solving, original and innovative thinking, and artistically, to name a few. Describe how you express your creative side.

PIQ #2 (Creative Side)

When I'm on the tennis court, I use my creative side to successfully defeat my opponent. I'll watch how the ball lands on one side, and strategically envision how I can powerfully return it. If a player approaches me on a certain side, I creatively envision which technique I'll employ. And, when our team is set to compete against another school, I analyze my opponent's moves to understand their strengths and weaknesses, so I can envision how I can out-maneuver them on the court. In each instance, I arrive on the court ready, because I've relied on my creative mind to mentally envision outcomes.

When I'm outside the court, I also tap into my creative side. Whether I'm building a structure for a class project, using spatial dimensions to place objects on a poster board, or planning out a chemical reaction in a Chemistry assignment, I creatively envision how I can approach each task. I can "see" the finished product in my mind, and this helps me to begin building each component. For example, in AP Calculus, I envision several potential formulas to approach a particular problem set. I imagine plugging in variables to each formula, helping me identify a potential solution. Using creative envisioning, I can eliminate variables and identify alternate solutions that may also apply.

In an artistic setting, I use creative envisioning in my art class. I envision the artistic form, and then envision all elements that create the form. I imagine the colors, texture, and dimensions, to bring my work to life. I often start with smaller components, and slowly build up to the final product.

Lastly, I use creative envisioning on a personal level. Whether my goal is to improve my grade in a class, write an exceptional paper, or support my team members on a collaborative project, I plug into this talent to help me envision the end goal. I will continue to rely on my creative side, envisioning outcomes, throughout my undergraduate studies. I believe this creative skill will help me succeed as a scholar, sports team member, and in my personal goals.

My Commentary

This essay was successfully executed because the writer utilized a consistent thread throughout. While focusing on her creative talent, she consistently mentions her ability to "see" or envision an outcome. She referenced this "envisioning" skill on the tennis court, in her AP Chemistry and AP Calculus courses, in her art class, and in her personal life. She walked us through her creative process by sharing vivid details. She convinced us that this talent will definitely come into play as an undergraduate at her future UC campus. She nailed it!

PIQ #2 (Creative Side)

When I was 10 years old, my passion for science and technology began developing. My earliest memory was when I teamed up with my cousin to build and program a robot with Legos. Conceptualizing, designing, and building innovative products is how I express my creative side.

Throughout high school I've participating in many technologically creative activities. For example, I participated in a community college program called "Technovation" where I learned how to code in Java and C++ during their coding Dojo. As part of a team of 5, we were given a "global challenge for entrepreneurship." Using the MIT App Inventor platform, we created an app to solve a problem in our community entitled, "Know What You're Eating!" This app identified chemicals and vitamins in food products, as well as alternatives to unhealthy foods.

I also expressed my creativity through the UC Santa Cruz Youth Empowerment Institute (YEI) Girls Coding Camp. At this camp, I designed an Apple Store app about food and environmental health using C++. And, this year I enrolled in a robotics course to learn about the use of robots today and how they are innovating the medical field. In this course we are designing a robot for the VEX Robot Competition. In teams of 4 we build robots for weekly tasks. Using C++ and Java we program robots, use a 3D printer, and create wood engravings with a robotic arm.

Lastly, I participated in a competition at UC Santa Cruz, sponsored by MESA (Mathematics, Engineering, Science Achievement). In this competition I designed a 3-D heart, complete with all chambers that illustrated blow flow, labeled important vessels, and illustrated exchange of oxygen and carbon dioxide.

Throughout all of these activities, I have expressed my creativity and innovative strength by writing code, designing a 3-D model heart, and constructing a fully functional robot. When I am in this creative and technical mode, I feel empowered to design or conceptualize innovative products to change the world. As a future undergraduate student, I intend to bring my passion for technology as I venture into my new University of California campus.

My Commentary

This essay rocks because the student didn't "dumb down" her language or examples. She embraced her love of STEM related activities and chose clever examples to showcase her creative talent. She focused on the innovative and problem-solving aspect of creativity – carefully choosing examples of coding, building robots, creating an app, designing robots and a 3D heart. We believe in her spirit of innovative creativity and have no doubt she will thrive in a rigorous academic institution. She rocks and she nailed it!

PIQ #3 *What would you say is your greatest talent or skill? How have you developed and demonstrated that talent over time?*

PIQ #3 (Greatest Talent)

I set five alarm clocks every night to ensure I get up at 3:00am. Because of the noise level in our home, I am unable to concentrate. It's not because I have problems concentrating or focusing, it's because we don't have a traditional home. My bedroom is our laundry room, and my sibling's bedroom is the garage. Therefore, I wake up early to spend quality time reading, writing, and completing assignments. I'd rather focus my energies this way, versus struggling every night with the noise of the TV and family discussions. This level of dedication to my studies – my work ethic – is my greatest talent.

My work ethic doesn't end once I leave my home in the morning. After completing my studies, I drive myself to school at 7:00am. On Monday's I take an IB course, Theory of Knowledge that ends at 6pm. From there I drive to another city to attend a one-year intensive college-admission program, and I'm home by 8pm. On other days of the week I'm participating in AVID until 6pm, followed by an Internship at Tri-City

Medical. Lastly, on Fridays I begin my 3-day work week, working 16 hours from Friday through Sunday as a server at Tei Café. Juggling all of this, with seasonal sports including Water Polo and Swim, while maintaining a 4.02 GPA.

I'm not sharing this information to elicit sympathy. Rather, I'm sharing this information to highlight the fire I have in myself to become an academic scholar. Sometimes I feel fatigued and drained, but I remind myself that being a first-generation student isn't easy. I must work twice as hard to achieve my college goals because I don't have the same level of guidance as others. I also remind myself that this trait – my strong work ethic – is going to aid me during my challenges at a University of California campus.

My Commentary

It's crazy this student could pack so much information into 310 words! She nailed it because she provides plenty of details to help us look inside her world. Her list of activities helps us understand what she's working with – a packed schedule of academics, internships, sports, and even working 16 hours each weekend. But, she balances this by sharing her 4.02 GPA and reminding us it was her strong work ethic (her greatest talent) that aided her success. Her closing is also very strong. She tells her reader she's not looking for sympathy. Instead, she shares her obstacles to let them to know she's not afraid of hard work. Bottom line, she's got what it takes to get through any rigorous challenge the UC's throw at her! #NailedIt

PIQ #3 (Greatest Talent)

I strive to be the best in everything I do – whether it is sports, academics, extracurricular activities, or even hobbies. I've always challenged myself to score the highest, reach the most challenging goals, or to simply improve. However, this competition is rarely against others. It is mostly against myself – for my best win, my best score, and my greatest improvement. My competitive spirit is my greatest talent and it has helped me succeed in my academic, athletic, and personal goals.

Academically, I've consistently challenged myself. I have always invested time and energy to improve my understanding of the subject or to master concepts. For example, I became determined to excel in AP Calculus. I spent additional time studying different concepts. This additional effort paid off, as I received one of the top three scores in a comprehensive math exam in AP Calculus. By placing in the top three, I was nominated to compete in a county-wide Mathletics Competition. Representing my high school in this competition gave me the opportunity to demonstrate my skills, and helped me develop confidence.

Aside from academics, I've also pushed myself to excel in sports. This competitive spirit allowed me to receive Most Valuable Player (MVP) last year, as well as 2-time All-League Basketball Team, and All County Team last year. Sports are not only a physical game but a mental puzzle. Championships aren't based solely on talent, but strategizing offensive moves to predict and counter opponent's future moves. Every play matters and requires critical thinking by studying opponent's weaknesses and strengths. Pushing myself physically is how I compete to improve my mental and physical game.

In the larger context, my competitive spirit compels me to pursue long term career goals. These include obtaining a 4-year college degree, attending graduate school, and returning to the Salinas Valley to represent Latinos in a positive way. With my competitive spirit and hard work ethic, I am confident I can achieve all of my goals – whether they are academic, athletic, or educational.

My Commentary

This essay is awesome because our student was challenged with a very difficult balancing act. She was challenged with describing her competitive spirit without coming across as boastful or arrogant. She nailed it by explaining that her competitive spirit was not an aggressive competition with others. Instead, she defines it as a competition with herself.

In carefully crafted language, she conveys a tone of pride as she triumphed in academic, athletic, and personal goals. She utilized the tip shared in Chapter 10 – how to showcase accomplishments without sounding arrogant. #NailedIt!

PIQ #4 *Describe how you have taken advantage of a significant educational opportunity or worked to overcome an educational barrier you have faced.*

PIQ #4 – Took Advantage of Education Opportunity

My father only finished grade school in Mexico and my mother only completed high school in the U.S. Because neither parent has attended college, I have had to figure out this process on my own. Furthermore, as the oldest of 5 children, I feel it is my responsibility to get through this process so I can help my younger siblings. Not having help at home, I took advantage of 3 significant educational opportunities that have helped me become a competitive candidate for college.

First, I joined AVID in the 8th grade. Through this program, I learned collaboration skills, organizational skills, and how to research colleges. AVID also provided me with SAT test preparation, tutors, and fee waivers. Through their help, I have been able to maintain a strong GPA, enroll in challenging courses, and be on the road toward applying to colleges.

Next, I joined Educational Talent Search (ETS) in my junior year. In ETS, they provided me with scholarship information, provided fee waivers, SAT practice tests, financial aid help, field trips, and career resources. Through their help, I have expanded my knowledge of the financial aid process. I doing so, I learned about colleges that meet full or partial financial need – including the UC's Blue and Gold Program.

Lastly, in my junior year, I applied and was accepted to the Quetzal Mama Scholars Program. In this free program, I have been part of a cohort of students where we learned about college entrance exams (including SAT Subject Tests and ACT), the UC application and personal statements, and scholarships. My participation in this program helped me become a more confident college applicant.

In these 3 programs I learned a lot. I learned how to stay on top of college deadlines, what colleges looks for, and how to prepare strategically. Most importantly, I learned to seek out help at a critical time, to positively impact my college goals.

My Commentary

This student strategically uses the first paragraph to provide some background context to help the UC people understand her starting point. Then, she methodically takes us through each of the 3 programs, explaining what she got out of them. What's clever about this essay is that the writer conveys a very strategic approach to the opportunities she has pursued. It's not at all random. It gives readers a glimpse into how she might navigate future challenges or obstacles. In closing, she tells them the gist of how the programs helped her. But, she also emphasizes how she took initiative to create the kind of future she wants. #NailedIt

PIQ #4 (Overcome Educational Barrier)

Coming to this country undocumented at the age of 10 years old, I experienced significant setbacks and challenges. Not understanding the language, not having resources, and needing to be invisible, were significant challenges. However, I was determined to succeed and I made up my mind that I would achieve my academic goals.

For example, in the 6th grade, I was placed in ELD classes. I was determined to master the complex English language. I was also determined to master English because my ELD status impacted my placement in mathematics. It was difficult for me to understand how I couldn't advance in mathematics, due to my language ability. This added yet another dimension to my desire to master English. In one year, I received a bilingual certificate and by 8th grade I was already in Honors English. I overcame this obstacle by spending several hours a night studying the language, watching television programs with subtitles, and practicing speaking with native English speakers. My commitment and determination to master the English language paid off. As of today, I am enrolled or have completed AP Language & Composition and AP English Literature.

In addition to being committed and determined to achieve excellence in mastering the English language, I also strive for academic excellence in all disciplines. For example, I set out a goal for myself to complete at least 8 Advanced Placement courses by my graduation date. As of today, I am enrolled or have completed 9 AP courses, including some of the most rigorous courses (AP Physics). I am passionate about challenging myself intellectually and striving for academic excellence.

Lastly, as an undocumented student I've refused to let my status hinder my future college goals. Instead, I've focused my energies and resources toward preparing myself to be as competitive, prepared, and knowledgeable as possible, so that I may thrive at my future University of California campus.

My Commentary

This essay works because the student avoided the mistake of the *Womp Womp* Essay. She avoided falling into the Victim Zone by adequately describing her challenge, but then flipping it and showcasing the positive outcomes. While she has incredible obstacles – such as being undocumented, an English Learner, and being placed in low level math due to her language challenges, she shows us how she easily navigated through triumphantly. She nailed it!

PIQ #5 *Describe the most significant challenge you have faced and the steps you have taken to overcome this challenge. How has this challenge affected your academic achievement?*

PIQ #5 (Most Significant Challenge)

When I was 6 years old, my family's doctor prescribed an ADHD medication that negatively affected me and significantly slowed my thought process. Because my parents didn't speak English, they couldn't explain to the doctor the terrible effect of this medication. I suffered immensely during the 6 years I took this intense drug. It wasn't until the 5th grade that I decided to stop the medication completely. However, without medication to cope with ADHD, it has been extremely difficult to complete timed exams or timed activities during high school. This challenge has affected my academic achievement in many ways.

Because I never received a documented IEP, I was ineligible to receive an accommodation for more time. This impacted me once I began taking Advanced Placement courses in my sophomore year. I could not request additional time to complete my quizzes, projects, or examinations. Even worse, I did not receive additional time to take AP exams. Yet, through hard work and commitment, I completed 5 AP courses while maintaining a 3.8 GPA and a class rank of #17.

To overcome my focus-related challenge, I did several things to achieve my academic goals. I scheduled time to speak with teachers each semester, explaining my challenge and requesting additional time for mid-terms, or quizzes. I also attended after-school tutoring every week to thoroughly understand content before advancing to another concept. Additionally, I spent several hours each day, reviewing lessons on Khan Academy.

Lastly, I used inspirational resources to help me stay focused on my goals. For example, in my "bible," Malcolm Gladwell's book, "David & Goliath" he talks about advantages of disadvantages of a disability, and how many world leaders and entrepreneurs have succeeded not in spite of their disability, but because of it. This concept of an advantage due to a disadvantage has inspired me to see my disability in a different way. Today I view my disability as a gift that increased my endurance, creativity, and resourcefulness. I now feel empowered that my disability is actually the sling in my hand, that may ultimately be my most powerful weapon.

My Commentary

This is one of my all-time favorite essays. Ever. I love this essay because this student's spirit and determination are flying off the charts! He fully describes his obstacle, then takes it further by describing how he navigated this challenge. In doing so, we learn how incredibly bright, resourceful, and determined he is. And, we learn a lot about his personality and life perspective. He flips the script by saying his disability is actually his most powerful weapon! Who does that? He also displays an incredible spirit of gratitude. Any other student could have conceded defeat and given up. Not this guy. The UC people must have wondered, "If this guy can flip a disability like this, with extraordinary outcomes, imagine what he can do at our UC campus?" #Nailed It.

PIQ #5 (Most Significant Challenge)

When I began elementary school, I felt lost. I didn't speak a word of English. Unfortunately, my mom didn't put me in preschool or kindergarten, so when I began 1st grade I was unprepared. One day, my teacher pulled me out of class and explained she was recommending I enroll in a summer writing program that would improve my English skills. Up to that point, I rarely spoke. My fluency in English was so terrible I couldn't even pronounce the simplest phrases. Learning English was one of the greatest challenges I've had in my lifetime.

To improve my skills, I started reading chapter books and reaching milestones. By

5th grade, I became one of the highest performing students. By time I got to middle school, I tested out of remedial English. But, my goal was not just to pass an exam, it was to write exceptional essays and compete with the top students. I began challenging myself in high school by taking Honors English courses where I learned how to write beyond basic components and to express myself creatively.

In my Junior year, I took my AP English Composition and received a B+. I learned different ways to write sentence structure, how to format an essay, and rhetorical devices. As a senior, I am now enrolled in AP Literature and earning an A grade. I'm learning more complex forms of English, and the historical forms of English literature.

Having moved so far beyond ELD English, and now taking AP English Literature, I have surpassed one of the biggest challenges in my lifetime. Having overcome this obstacle, I have learned patience. It takes a long time to master a concept and being patient is critical to achieving long-term goals. Secondly, I learned to believe in myself to become a confident writer. Lastly, I learned to ask for help and develop a network of resources. I now believe that I can accomplish so much more, and I'm looking forward to using my patience, confidence, and ability to seek resources as an incoming student at the University of California.

My Commentary

Do you see how this student followed the instructions and named the struggle? But, she also followed the secondary instructions which were to describe the steps she took to overcome the challenge *and* how it affected her academic achievement. She does this straight out of the gate by telling you where she started (Kindergarten) and her uphill battle with learning English. Then she takes you through the steps she took to help her become successful. Lastly, she ties this together with her subsequent academic achievement – where she received A grades in AP Literature. She went full circle. Now, if she just told you she got an A in AP Literature, it wouldn't be so impressive. However, we know her starting point because she wrote an effective introduction. More importantly, she tells us the top 3 things she got from navigating this challenge: She learned patience; gained confidence; and learned how to identify resources. Those are pretty good qualities for a UC candidate! She nailed it.

PIQ #6   *Think about an academic subject that inspires you. Describe how you have furthered this interest inside and/or outside of the classroom.*

PIQ #6 (Favorite Academic Subject)

Last year, the Intern Coordinator from Congressmen Doug Applegate (49th District) came to present to our AP Government class. Something she said resonated with me deeply. She said, "If you want to see the change, you have to be the change." Her message was about "flipping" the 49th district" from Republican (and strong Trump supporter) Congressman Darryl Issa. This internship proved to be a huge deal at my high school campus, where half of the study body is split between Applegate and Issa supporters. After her speech, I decided to apply for an internship in Applegate's office. This internship opened my eyes to the fascinating discipline of Political Science.

Throughout my internship, I attended the Progressive Democrats meeting, where I saw first-hand how the political process is emotional and fast-moving, even on the State level. I saw people running around, debating and pursuing endorsements, and I pictured myself in that arena. I wanted to be there, as part of our American political system.

Because of my excitement to be involved in the political process, I founded the first partisan club at my campus – the Democratic Club, chartered by the California Young Democrats. As President of this club, I organized a voter registration drive, educated students about age restrictions and where they can vote (local, state or federal levels), and coordinated local efforts. I was invited to the 2017 California Young Democrat retreat in Lake Tahoe where I listened to candidates speak and observed representatives from the Latino Caucus, Environmental Caucus, and the Women's Caucus. I was also able to vote for my choice of Governor, Lieutenant Governor, Attorney General, and Secretary of State. I was one of only 2 high school students attending, where all other attendees were adults and college students.

These experiences have solidified my desire to pursue Political Science as my undergraduate major. My long-term goal is to serve as a Legislative Aide at the State Capitol because I'm passionate about criminal justice and reform. I look forward to learning Political Science theories, joining Young Democrats and other political organizations as an undergraduate scholar.

My Commentary

This prompt nails almost all of the strategies we've discussed in this book. The student starts out with an effective quote that's short and sweet, and ends the essay referring back to the quote (full circle). This is a highly effective essay because she describes how her interest in Political Science was ignited and how it evolved. You can feel her enthusiasm as she discusses interesting details. Finally, it's clear her exposure within the arena of politics led to her decision to major in Political Science. Nailed it!

PIQ #6 (Favorite Academic Subject)

This past September, and in response to Trump's DACA repeal, I coordinated a demonstration in front of my school's flagpole. Because many of my close friends, relatives, and peers are undocumented, this was very personal to me. I showed up in my "resist" t-shirt and gave a speech to 50 students to discuss their rights under DACA, increase morale, and prevent a walk-out at our high school. I have always been interested in politics, with the goal of becoming a California Senator. Because of my background, upbringing, acute political awareness, and interest in politics, Political Science is my favorite subject.

As a politically astute student, I still wear my "Bernie for President" t-shirt, recalling when Senator Sanders visited our high school campus. I follow many political issues on NPR, social media, listen to podcasts such as Malcolm Gladwell's Revisionist History, and read books in my spare time like "*Lies my Teacher Told Me.*" However, I also make a point to watch conservative networks to understand alternate perspectives. The topic of Political Science fascinates me and has compelled me to take courses such as AP US History, IB History of the Americas, and AP European History.

As a Political Scientist, I was thrilled to be accepted to the Chicano/Latino Youth Leadership Project (CLYLP) in Sacramento. At this week-long conference, I networked with other Chicanx/Latinx students from across California, visited the State Capitol, and participated in a Mock Hearing on the Assembly floor. Additionally, I was elected by my peers to serve as Southern California Ambassador. My participation in this program helped me learn more about the political process in California.

Whether I am hosting a DACA demonstration in front of my school, participating in a Mock Hearing on the Assembly Floor at the State Capitol, or learning political theories in IB History of the Americas, I continually challenge myself to learn more about the discipline of Political Science.

My Commentary

First, she comes right out of the gate identifying her politics. That's completely fine. She also puts it out there – that she's got her hopes set on becoming a California Senator. All good stuff. She does a fantastic job describing how she furthered her interest in Political Science inside and outside of the classroom. In fact, she uses the Magical Power of 3 to provide three great examples, backing up her claim that Political Science is the academic subject that inspires her. However, what is most impressive about her writing is the tone. She is not apologetic for her political position and her examples convey a spirited political warrior! #NailedIt

PIQ #6 (Favorite Academic Subject)

Beginning in elementary school, I developed a love of mathematics. I was on the Math Olympiad Team, learning and teaching math strategies through competition. This experience was extremely fun because it allowed me to open my mind to creatively solve problems, explore alternate methods, and learn new math concepts.

Unlike politics, where there are many angles and perspectives, math is different. In math, everyone speaks the same language. While there are different routes or methods to get to the solution, the answer will always be the same. It's like a puzzle, where the answer (or big picture) will eventually come into focus. But, it's the journey of finding the answer that's the most gratifying. I can write a full page of steps, involving every math strategy spanning Geometry to Calculus, just to yield one answer. Getting to the answer is the sweet part.

Because of my passion for mathematics, I have challenged myself with the most difficult math classes including AP Calculus AB and AP Calculus BC. In these classes, I got to learn things like how bumble bees construct their hives using hexagons, maximizing volume and minimizing wax. Outside of the classroom, I also challenge myself by teaching mathematics to my peers. I tutor my peers who are struggling with AP Calculus, and who doubt their ability to perform mathematics.

I have furthered my interest in math outside of the classroom in different ways. For example, I often visit Khan Academy for fun, and to and review lesson plans to gain a different perspective. Recently, I visited the site to explore Differential Calculus because I was interested in limits, continuity, derivatives, and derivative applications.

Whether I am competing in a math competition, tutoring my peers in math, or solving a complex math problem, I am doing the most enjoyable thing – learning about math. Because mathematics is my favorite subject, I decided to pursue a career as a mathematics professor. Toward this goal, I look forward to learning more about Applied Mathematics at the University of California.

My Commentary

First off, we totally get this student absolutely loves math. There's no question. She does this by sharing different contexts where she's pursued her math interest – Math Olympiad, tutoring her peers, visiting Khan Academy, and taking the most rigorous mathematics courses available to her. She also conveys her love of math through the analogy of a puzzle and how math is like a game. The concept of a math as a fun game could only be described by someone who truly loves math. She ends her essay connecting her passion of math with her major and her intended career goal. #NailedIt

PIQ #7 *What have you done to make your school or your community a better place?*

PIQ #7 (Made my Community a Better Place)

I think the more we serve our community, the more relationships we build, and that these relationships can impact others in a profound way. I have always believed it is my responsibility to serve others, in as many ways as I can. To date, I have served more than 120 hours in my local community, through five different service organizations.

Starting as a Freshman, I began volunteering at the Saint Vincent DePaul Thrift Shop in downtown Fallbrook. In this role, I sort items, price them, and translate for customers in Spanish. I am proud of this role, as these low-cost items are available for people in my community who cannot afford to shop at traditional shops.

Next, I began volunteering at the MAAC Head Start Program. In this role, I helped teachers with activities, songs, and crafts for pre-schoolers. In this role, I believe I was helping students gain a positive experience about school, and therefore getting them excited about their transition to Kindergarten. This is an important investment as I believe education is a critical resource.

In addition to helping younger students, I am also helping older students. I have served as a Teen Group Advisor for the Fallbrook Pregnancy Center. This organization is funded by Planned Parenthood, and helps young men and women learn about reproductive options and sexual education. Because there is a large prevalence of teen pregnancy in my city, I believe I am serving an important function.

Lastly, I serve youth in my community by teaching them how to cook and prepare nutritious meals. I volunteer at my local library and teach elementary school kids how to make things like pita pockets, yogurt parfaits, and peanut butter rolls. This is fun because I am teaching children how to eat well at a young age, so they set this foundation for later in life.

Whether I am working in a Thrift Shop, advising teens on pregnancy issues, helping preschools become excited about school, or helping elementary students learn about healthy food options, I am making my community a better place. I look forward to serving others in my new UC undergraduate campus.

My Commentary

The beauty of this essay is the way the student strategically describes each service activity. Instead of simply stating her position and describing her duties, she talks about the *impact*. That extra *impact* sentence following each description helps the reader understand her motivation, convictions, and purpose for service. More importantly, it makes it evident she understands the bigger picture – how her work ultimately benefits her community. It's clear she didn't pick these service opportunities randomly, trying to check off boxes on her application. Her descriptions make us believe she strategically chose these activities because she believes in the value and impact of service. #NailedIt

PIQ #7 (Made Community Better Place)

When I was 8 years old, I had the opportunity to read Catherine Ryan Hyde's "Pay It Forward." Reading this book helped develop my mentality of "paying it forward" and viewing my potential to create a positive impact on my community. This mentality compelled me to serve in various roles including serving as a band mentor, a math tutor to elementary students, a writing tutor at my school's writing center, and a one-on-one coach for students learning English as a Second Language. In each of these mentorship roles I have been able to make a positive impact on my community by investing my time and energy towards future generations.

For example, as a band mentor, I've been able to pass down my knowledge for success to aspiring musician thus helping further their love and aspiration for music. Similarly, as a math/homework tutor at Alvin Dunn Elementary School, I created creative ways to help students learn and get motivated about math including creating flash cards and worksheets. Additionally, through being a writing tutor at my high school, I have helped students develop and refine their thoughts in essays to help them succeed in English and History.

Recently, through the Writing Center, I have invested two hours per week teaching a class of English Learners at my high school. In this role, I help them strengthen their English writing and speaking skills, directing them toward increased language fluency and analytical writing. Although many of my service opportunities have been through one-on-one service, I am confident the people I've helped will continue to "pay it forward."

From these experiences, I have grown in many ways. I have improved my interpersonal communication skills, facilitated student learning, and helped students view education more positively. This has taught me that my service has a direct and positive influence, that can be passed down to others. Aligned with Hyde's message, I feel like I've left a positive imprint of goodness within my community, even if it's in a small way.

My Commentary

This essay works because the writer begins by telling us how her spirit of service began. She relates it to a book she read – inspiring her to "pay it forward." She nails it because she shares details of where and *how* she paid it forward (using examples of Band Mentor, Homework Tutor, and Writing Center Tutor). Most importantly, she tells us what she got out of this service. She tells us what she learned, and how she benefitted from serving others. Nailed it!

PIQ #8 *Beyond what has already been shared in your application, what do you believe makes you stand out as a strong candidate for admissions to the University of California?*

PIQ #8 (Standout Candidate)

My parents were born in a poor village in Oaxaca, Mexico. Lacking formal education, they worked as dishwashers, book factory assemblers, and picked grapes. Growing up in the East Side of San José, I attended a low-performing high school where only 82% of students graduate, and two thirds do not meet A-G requirements. However, I feel blessed that my parents instilled in me the spirit of *ganas*. I believe this quality makes me a stand out candidate.

This spirit compelled me to accomplish extraordinary things. For example, in middle school I wanted to advance in my favorite subject – mathematics. I enrolled in the José Valdes Math Institute, spending 3 summers, 7 hours a day, for 8 weeks each summer, learning algebra strategies. While most kids would never volunteer to spend summers studying math, I was determined to get ahead. Completing this program helped me advance into higher level math, achieving my goal of completing both sections of AP Calculus by my junior year.

The spirit of *ganas* also helped me excel in STEM related coursework. I took every AP STEM related course available to me including AP Chemistry, AP Physics, AP Calculus (AB & BC), and AP Statistics. Outside of high school, I challenged myself by taking Fundamentals of Chemistry at a Community College, earning an A grade.

My mindset of *ganas* also helped me excel outside the classroom. I have participated in every STEM related program available to me, including serving as President of MESA, member of SHPE, and completing COSMOS at UC Santa Cruz.

Lastly, having *ganas* pushed me to participate in programs for first generation students. I participated for 2 years in AVID, Puente, and the Goodwill Assets Program, learning organizational skills, college research skills, and test preparation. One of the most important programs I participated in was the Quetzal Mama UC Essay Writing Boot Camp. In this camp, I learned how to identify my strengths, analyze the prompts, and to tell my story. Although I am confident, intelligent, and hardworking, I believe my spirit of *ganas* is what makes me stand out as an exceptional candidate.

My Commentary

The first obvious observation is that this student could have easily responded to several of the other PIQ prompts. He could have responded to the "Greatest Talent or Skill" prompt, or the "Educational Opportunity" prompt. However, he had already written about these topics so he decided to claim his "stand out" status by talking about his spirit of *ganas*. He nailed it!

Do you notice how every paragraph discusses a challenge or obstacle, but he quickly addresses the challenge and states the actions he took to overcome the challenge? By doing this, his action-oriented, can-do, create my own future qualities really shine through. He used the "flip it" strategy we discussed in Chapter 8 (*Tu Voz*).

He also does a wonderful job referring to specific programs and resources. He doesn't simply say, "I participated in a few programs." He names the programs. That's important because the UC people are aware of competitive programs like COSMOS and CLYLP.

Lastly, every one of his 5 paragraphs convey a very assertive and confident tone. We believe in this student because he has convinced us he can create miracles out of nothing! #Nailed It.

PIQ #8 (Standout Candidate)

Aside from my strong academic profile, my 120+ hours of service to my community, and my passion for biological sciences, I believe I have much more to offer my future classmates at the University of California. I believe I am a standout candidate because of my strong cultural authenticity.

I am extremely proud of my heritage and roots and believe my experiences will benefit my future classmates. I have an exceptional understanding of the history, language, foods, religious events, holidays, and festivities of the Mexican culture. Because of this, I believe I can add an interesting perspective to share with my future classmates.

For example, I am President of the *Club Futuro*. In this club, we host cultural events to promote the Latino culture at my high school campus. For example, we performed at festivals, fundraised for food drives, hosted *Dia de los Muertos* festivals, and facilitated guest speakers during Hispanic Heritage Month. These activities allowed me to share my Mexican culture with all of my classmates

I am also a member of my high school campus' Ballet Folklorico. In this group we perform various regions including Jalisco, Chiapas, Sinaloa, and San Luis Potosi. By performing, we are teaching others about traditions and history of Mexico. Through dance, I am sharing much about our rich history, politics, and culture.

Lastly, I embrace my culture as a volunteer in the GANAS after school program. GANAS stands for Guide, Advise, Nurture And Support. This program serves Latino students aged 9-14 from low-income neighborhoods. GANAS allows me the opportunity to mentor young Latino students, helping them develop leadership skills and positive decision-making skills.

Whether I am adding rich conversations about Mexican or Latin American history, or sharing the tradition of dance or food, or empowering younger Latinos in my community, I believe my cultural authenticity is a unique quality that makes me a standout candidate for the University of California. (317 words)

My Commentary

This student used this prompt wisely. The concept of "cultural authenticity" is not really aligned with any of the other prompts. However, this student uses the opportunity to speak about her rich heritage. She recognizes that cultural authenticity is a valuable trait and used 317 words to describe how she embraces her culture. She also tells the UC's why this quality would be beneficial at a UC campus. This student uses wonderful examples to convey her strong and positive identity as a Latina. This identity is believable because she provides multiple contexts, over a long period of time. #NailedIt

I hope you enjoyed reading Nailed It! 2 and learning Quetzal Mama's 7 Steps to Nail your PIQ's.

Let me know if you used these essay-writing tools and received admission to your #1 UC campus!

If you enjoyed this book, you'll love the other 4 Quetzal Mama books available on Amazon and Barnes & Noble.

Learn up-to-date admission strategies via monthly blog articles at quetzalmama.com/blog.

If you want additional strategies and insider tips about the UC's or other competitive college campuses, bring Quetzal Mama (Dr. Roxanne Ocampo) to your high school campus!

Contact us directly at

quetzalmama@gmail.com

Connect with us:

www.quetzalmama.com

facebook.com/quetzalmama

@QuetzalMama (Twitter) / @quetzalmama (Instagram)